Inspired Learning: 50 Insights from Personal Transformative Learning Journeys

Published in the United States of America by
University of Central Oklahoma.
100 N University Drive
Edmond, OK, 73034

FIRST EDITION

Front cover image by Beth Bolding.

ISBN- 9781086834277

DEDICATION

This book is dedicated
to all learners and especially to
three educator scholars, who made
lifelong learning their personal commitment
and who inextricably advanced transformative learning
in institutional practice and through administrative leadership.

Dr. J. Gail Neely, *UCO Award Benefactor since 1999*
For stewardship and vision to establish an award for teaching excellence
and to be present annually for leading luncheon conversations and
encouraging us to "think."

Dr. Don Betz, *UCO President from 2011-2019*
For leadership and a consistent enthusiasm for the excellence in teaching
award as well as the learning conversations among recipients.

Dr. John F. Barthell, *UCO Provost since 2013*
For encouraging this book project and for seeing the potential benefits of
the book as a platform for learners to hear from truly inspired educators.

TABLE OF CONTENTS

PART I: Coming to Learn: Cultivating a "No-Gritch" Mentality

IN HONOR OF
DR. J. GAIL NEELY

December 10, 1939 ~ August 20, 2017

FOREWORD FROM DR. J. GAIL NEELY

Dr. Neely shaped this book's direction; he received early drafts of contributor essays and crafted the following Foreword prior to his passing.

***

What happens when curiosity and will power meet learning disability? Briefly, I will explain.

Learning Disability

Early in grade school, I discovered I had serious limitations: 1) I could not read aloud. Reading silently to myself was just fine. 2) I could not memorize things. 3) I was an extremely slow reader—one word at a time.

Rapidly, I developed an attitude that most of my teachers were arbitrary and capricious. I discovered that to keep them off me, I had to do excellent work. Consequently, my determination to overcome my problems was enhanced.

One example of my interactions with teachers was as a first grader when I was asked to grade the second grader's papers. I did not know any of the answers no matter how hard I tried, and I began to cry. My teacher asked me why I was crying. Then, she said she had forgotten to give me the key and to instruct me on how to use it. Another example is when I was forbidden to use a regular pencil to write in cursive; instead, I was given a large awkward pencil and told I must print with it without a satisfactory answer as to why.

When I was 2–4 years old, my dad was in the South Pacific in World War II. I eventually felt like I was an adult at 2 years of age and 100 years old at age 10.

My Abilities

I was insatiably curious. I could think. Rote memory was nearly impossible for me; however, if I could derive the information from stringing facts together, or if the item was funny, I had it forever.

I had a very strong will ("hardheaded" some might say) and was determined to conquer these problems. When challenged, I would attack. To solve my problem(s), I had to derive creative ways to accomplish the task. The reality of failure was not embraced; I knew I could succeed if I went at it correctly.

Mentors

Extremely important to me were gentle inputs from my mentors: my father, mother, grocery store owner, clarinet teacher and other select teachers.

My father only had a high school diploma. However, each night he would study by himself; I watched. His self-study taught him mechanics, then algebra and trigonometry, metallurgy, lasers, and precision measurement. Ultimately, he went from a mechanic shop foreman to function as a consulting engineer at the Tinker Air Force base in the precision instrument laboratory. However, he could not hold a title even as an engineering assistant because of a lack of formal education. He was a constant inspiration.

Extremely important to me were gentle inputs from my mentors: my father, mother, grocery store owner, clarinet teacher and other select teachers. My father only had a high school diploma. However, each night he would study by himself; I watched.

My mother had graduated from Central State Normal School in Edmond, OK. After marriage, she turned her considerable skills to her family; she would not accept sloppy thinking.

The owner of a little one-room grocery store not far from our house had graduated in chemical engineering during the Great Depression. There were no jobs; so he started the little grocery. When I was a third grader, he would give me an algebra or chemistry problem and just enough instruction that I would work for hours/days to solve it. When I presented him with the answer, if correct, he would give me a candy and give me another problem. I loved this process, but I did not like how fuzzy my head felt while I was problem-solving.

When in the third grade, I decided to play the clarinet, but there was no one to teach me. I searched the small town of Edmond and found a junior high band director that was willing to let me try out for the junior high school band. If I could pass the audition, I could play with them. I learned to play with a brief instruction and from then on, I would walk a mile across the railroad tracks to the junior high and play with them. Ultimately, I became first chair clarinet and drum major. I also got a music scholarship to the University of Central Oklahoma until I had to let it go because biology and chemistry labs pushed out music labs.

Intermittently, a really great teacher would clarify something for me. Ultimately, I visited each one from grade school through medical school and told them how much they meant to me.

Overcoming Adversity

Self-study became my major problem-solving method. ***The key to self-study is to ask yourself questions.***

I taught myself to go to sleep within two minutes and wake fully in seconds. I practiced this on the floor when in high school. The reason? I felt that doctors would require those skills to be safe and productive.

I taught myself to "think read." Meaning, I would think about what a book, paper, etc. was attempting to tell. I then would rapid read to find the answer to my question. ***Asking myself questions*** became a way of life. This made reading very fast and comprehension almost complete.

I worked on memory so that I developed a psychological construct of what it was trying to convey, then I could derive the words on the fly. Ultimately, I became state champion in a traditional ceremony that required my speaking from memory for about an hour.

Career Development (I teach the same way, Socratically, and enjoy listening to minds work)

My curiosity drove my quest for knowledge, testing my knowledge against the universe of knowledge on the subject. Often, my asking what appeared to me to be fundamental to the topic would discover whole areas never explored. Just as often, when I would present an idea to get the missing information, people around me would put it down. Ultimately, I began to use the negative responses from others to be a sign that I was on the correct path.

Some discoveries doing this were: 1) cystic fibrosis patients

> *Soon, fear of failure begins to obstruct learning. Failure is a big important part of learning and freedom. It is important to be given the opportunity and to take the right to fail.*

known to have terrible sinus disease but interestingly little or no middle ear disease (common thought was that both should be severe—not so); 2) serial sections through acoustic tumors with the eighth nerve showed the unique relationship between the tumor and nerve of origin. There were no nerves passing the tumor, just a few dispersed nerve fibers; and 3) the inner ear and eighth nerve have heat shock proteins; we also defined where they are.

So, what is transformative learning? My own take on that is transforming from something external to something internal and intensely personal. Learning is fun, but not easy, and begins at birth, perhaps in utero. It begins very personal. Learning about gravity on a slightly sloping lawn or buoyancy in a shallow pool. The learner is the teacher.

Soon, fear of failure begins to obstruct learning. Failure is a big important part of learning and freedom. It is important to be given the opportunity and to take the right to fail. Unfortunately, well-meaning external environments begin to emphasize that failure is bad and should be avoided. Consequently, freedom is lost and learning degraded. One who seeks to appear wise is a fool. Embrace your ignorance, enjoy it, and learn from it. You only know you are making progress when you feel inadequate. However, it takes a while to overcome one's internal fears and the external surrounding environment misunderstanding of failure.

Always give your very best. If it is not good enough, so be it. That is all you have at the moment. If you give less than a 100% effort, then you do not know where you are. There is strength in not being enough. Improving is a power-giving option. Each time you succeed after failing, you get stronger and more confident.

> *Nothing is more stimulating and encouraging than success. We learn things two ways—intellectually and emotionally. Intellectual learning is rapid but tends to be external. Emotional learning takes longer, is personal, and can be refined.*

So, what should the target audience be? It is good to remember *when* we start learning. All of those are our target audience. Others can guide, but all should let learners solve their own problems, and fail. Encouragement and guidance can only be heard and understood when it is personal. It is helpful at times to set up a manageable project so that success is likely. Nothing is more stimulating and encouraging than success. We learn things two ways—intellectually and emotionally. Intellectual learning is rapid but tends to be external. Emotional learning takes longer, is personal, and can be refined.

It is hoped that the contents of this book will help define and give examples of how to learn transformatively, from external to internal and personal. The secret is asking yourself questions. By that, you focus on the question and not who is asking it. Compare your knowledge against the universe of knowledge on the topic, not the course, the book, or the teacher. Anything heard or read is just the tip of the iceberg; the great bulk is hidden below waiting for your discovery by asking yourself fundamental questions and seeking the answers.

Enjoy,
J (John) Gail Neely, M.D., FACS

J. GAIL NEELY

The late J. Gail Neely, M.D. (University of Oklahoma) had an insatiable curiosity about all things, especially in Otology and Neurotology. He served as Director of Otology and Neurotology at Washington University School of Medicine, where he directed the T32 physician training program for 19 years. He is a former chair of the Department of Otolaryngology at the University of Oklahoma where he served for 10 years. Neely advanced his learning through fellowships at the National Science Foundation and Yale University. His scholarly work resulted in more than 100 publications and many awards and honors. He was elected to the Baylor Hall of Fame in 2008 and to the University of Central Oklahoma's Luminary Society in 2015. He was named one of the "Best Doctors in America" for 23 consecutive years and was awarded Teacher of the Year numerous times by three different universities.

Editors' Note: Dr. Neely is the inspiration for this collection of essays. All contributors are recipients of the University of Central Oklahoma's Neely Excellence in Teaching Award, which Neely established to honor his mentors during his undergraduate work at UCO. Neely returned to UCO annually for the awards ceremony and luncheon to recognize each year's recipients. This book is the manifestation of his encouragement to capture the annual luncheon conversations for sharing with all those interested in teaching and learning. Neely remained at Washington University until 2016 when health issues demanded his retirement; he passed away on August 20, 2017.

ACKNOWLEDGMENTS

We are deeply indebted to Dr. Neely, whose 2011 St. Louis dinner invitation to Jeanetta and Ed is responsible for funded grants, publications, presentations, and the collegial relationship we now enjoy that is filled with research and editorial work capable of bringing a project like this to fruition.

Jeanetta and Ed are sincerely grateful to the gifted Anna Doré, who has become the presence that was missed in previous attempts to advance this project even as key others provided their assistance.

Many thanks as well to all of our Neely award recipients who graciously served as contributors and honored our deadline requests. Without your efforts, this book project would not exist.

We thank former Diverse Student Scholars research and editorial assistants (Ashley, Jacie, and Andi). Ashley Neese devoted much time and effort conducting photo shoots with contributors and editing photos distinctly for this project. Jacie Harvel and Andi Ullrich willingly served as student reviewers and offered feedback to contributors. We also appreciate our team of faculty reviewers who offered their valuable feedback to help each of our contributors improve their essays.

Along with Ashley Neese, we thank UCO Photographic Services, Craig Beuchaw, and Eriech Tapia for their assistance with capturing and editing additional contributor photos featured in the book.

Finally, we thank UCO executive leaders, Dr. Don Betz, Dr. John F. Barthell, Dr. Charlotte Simmons, Executive Director Anne Holzberlein, and President Patti Neuhold-Ravikumar, for their support of this project, of the university's commitment to transformative learning, and of the opportunity to showcase university faculty.

PREFACE

This work takes a personal approach to breaking down the transformative learning process. Through storytelling, 23 different professors—all recipients of the Neely Excellence in Teaching Award—share how they learned to learn. The 23 chapters cover foundational aspects of transformative learning through personal learning journeys in a way that is engaging, relatable, and unique to each author. A few chapters express the adversity faced by those learning or teaching in new countries and how beneficial it can be to the learner to become more open-minded to new experiences and cultures. Other chapters explain how personal challenges or positive mentorships completely changed their outlook about learning or teaching. Often the most transformative types of learning occurred through authors making mistakes, opening themselves to new opportunities, and maintaining a lifelong growth mindset. Though people might assume learning is the act of merely taking in knowledge, *Inspired Learning* shows just how rich the learning process can be and how far a transformative learning mindset can take both students and teachers.

OVERVIEW OF THE BOOK

Inspired Learning is divided into three parts: (1) Coming to Learn: Cultivating a "No-Gritch" Mentality; (2) You and Others: Without "We" There is Little Learning; and (3) Questioning Upside Down and Backwards: Thinking Differently about Learning. The three parts examine the learning process from the perspective of award-winning professors through their personal learning journeys.

Part One follows five professors as they used life experience, mentorship, and adversity to become better, more efficient learners and teachers. In *Chapter 1*, Anita Glee Bertram expresses her passion for the study of the process of aging and how it inspired her to incorporate service learning in her classroom, resulting in a synthesis of textbook concepts with real world experiences. In *Chapter 2*, Wei R. Chen explains how he brings his Chinese upbringing into his teaching through his respect, passion, and admiration for the profession. Jeanetta D. Sims reflects, in *Chapter 3,* on how her experiences as a dancer and scholar of color motivated her to create opportunities and resources for diverse student scholars at her university. *Chapter 4* discusses Gladys Lewis' Inside/Out learning method, capable of shaping transformative life attitudes through the combination of internal curiosity and external teaching. In *Chapter 5*, John F. Barthell was transformed through undergraduate research to see engagement with the subject beyond the given text as essential to the learning process and as a great way to become comfortable with uncertainty. In *Chapter 6*, highly accomplished Celloist and professor, Tess Remy-Shumacher, encourages learners to avoid an "easy way out" and to embrace failure as a part of growth. In *Chapter 7*, Cheryl B. Frech remembers how time and hard work has transformed her from a student with no concrete direction to a mentor in the science community, as well as a senior professor at UCO. In *Chapter 8,* Mohamed Bingabr describes how he came to the United States from Yemen, forcing him to adjust over time to the new learning processes, struggles, and cultural differences involved in being an international student. As the current chair of his department at UCO, he reflects on the value of studying abroad and how it expanded his mind on other cultures and contributed to his desire to teach.

In Part Two, contributors emphasize the importance of healthy learning environments, mentorship, and learning together. In *Chapter 9*, Robert Terrell shares his difficult past relationship with studying and how key people in his life helped him improve and transform his learning mindset. He now returns the favor to his students through his guidance and teaching methods which encourage growth. In *Chapter 10*, Robert Doan reflects on all of the important mentors in his life, and how they pushed him to become a better learner beyond what he ever thought was capable. In *Chapter 11*, Tawni Holmes talks about her life in academia, and how the bubble of higher education differs greatly from much of the outside world. The bubble she refers to is the environment of shared learning, independent thinking, and a strive for diversity. In *Chapter 12*, Kaye Sears discusses how moving around as a child helped her learn to become flexible and adaptable to new situations. She now mentors students in home economics the same way her own teachers mentored her to take on new experiences in a way that results in transformation and growth. In *Chapter 13*, Matthew Hollrah shares how he applies his parents' teaching techniques to his current classroom, which requires the learner to ask questions, lead discussions, and create opportunities to surprise themselves with their own discoveries. In *Chapter 14,* Christy Vincent expresses the importance of social support in learning environments to help students in varying circumstances find success.

Part Three tells personal stories of how different learners found themselves learning in better ways that may seem backwards or surprising to others. In *Chapter 15,* Daniel Vincent's "Aha!" teaching moment occurred when he realized the process of seeking is just as important as gaining a body of knowledge. Through embracing "Aha!" moments of realized ignorance, students and teachers can both better experience transformative learning. In *Chapter 16*, peer discussions, exploration into effective teaching practices, and a transformative change in mindset allowed David Bass to grow in his thinking on what makes a student successful in learning. In *Chapter 17*, Wayne Stein encourages learners to have the spirit of a warrior, which involves "dying daily" on a transformational path of growth. As a teacher, Stein uses storytelling and critical creativity to inspire development in his students. In *Chapter 18*, Joselina Cheng explains the importance of being a lifelong learner and how it can lead to self-actualization and fulfilment, as well as help people keep up with the constant shifts in technology and workplace environments. In *Chapter 19*, J. David Macey shares his experiences as a gay professor, and how being open with one's identity in the classroom can spark productive discussions and new understandings in what he refers to as an "uncomfortable but fruitful middle ground." In *Chapter 20*, J. Kole Kleeman expresses how he taught in the Department of American Studies and Mass Media at the University of Lodz, Poland as a Fulbright professor. Through his experience, he learned how to successfully apply for the Fulbright grant, and how to interact and connect with peers and students on an international level. In *Chapter 21*, Gloria Caddell compares her learning and teaching experience to that of a tree, with roots and leaves symbolizing the people and experiences that helped her grow. Through patient observation and student independence, Caddell encourages students to ask research questions that do not yet have answers to become well-rounded scientists and learners. In *Chapter 22*, Luis Montes encourages learners to go beyond what they see others do or think and allow themselves to add their own insights to each situation. Montes reminds teachers that they must learn from students and learn to approach things with inquisitive dissatisfaction. In *Chapter 23*, Laura Bolf-Beliveau recognizes the value of emotion in the classroom as a tool to create a third space where students feel safe and open to share their feelings in a way that promotes transformative learning.

INTRODUCTION

How often do we hear "how" others have learned? And, what are the personal stories of trial, challenge, failure, and success from those who have committed themselves to lifelong learning?

In this collection, excellent teachers reflect on their own transformative learning journeys. Through personal stories, this book offers a blend of voices filled with multiple perspectives on teaching, transformative learning, and scholarship that will inspire us all in our efforts to continue learning.

The book's structure emerged from the contributors' inspirational personal stories; contributors are award-winning educators from multiple fields including music, chemistry, engineering, communication, biology, marketing, nutrition, English, medicine, and accounting among others. Their essays capture critical learning reflections of the people, places, and happenings that prompted them to become passionate about learning. This learning transformation would lead them to become lifelong learners, to retain curiosity in their fields, and to eventually earn recognition for excellence in teaching.

Enjoy the book's structure with essays organized into three parts. In Part I, essays consider how we come to learn and the importance of cultivating a "no-gritch mentality."[1] Gritch refers to speech acts that include complaints, excuses, griping, blaming, and whining; a no-gritch mentality is a sign of resilience and steadfast persistence in learning. In Part II, essays affirm the importance of mentorship, personal relationships, and others in learning. In Part III, topics are explored related to questioning and thinking differently about learning.

For students, this book is a nudge to confidently undertake their own personal learning journeys. For faculty, this is encouragement to continue in the mindset of being a student. For all audiences, crucial lessons about learning emerge that prompt even more fundamental questions related to what constitutes transformative learning.

Insights for transformative learning permeate the pages ahead; these deliver on the promise of the book's title by collectively appearing in the conclusion. So, if you are the reader who skips to the back of the book or flips through to the middle for something that catches your attention, feel free to indulge.

PART I

Coming to Learn: Cultivating a "No-Gritch" Mentality

People often come to learning ill-prepared and lacking fortitude, despite having a unique set of strengths and capacities for learning. This section offers stories of curiosity, passion, and comfort for combatting adversities that arise while pursuing your learning journey.

CHAPTER ONE

Anita Glee Bertram, Ph.D.

Watch the Road Signs: Everyone is a Potential Guide to Learning

My Story

L earning has always been highly valued in my family. I grew up in a farm family with a wonderful mom and dad and two sisters. Neither of my parents had a college degree but they wanted more for their daughters. From the time I was little bitty, there was the understanding that although my parents had only what their farm could produce—cotton and cattle—their daughters would be given the opportunity to go to college. They scrimped and saved to make that happen. Also, we were taught that education was a privilege and we must take every advantage of every experience and learn from that opportunity. Our country school had only a few activities besides sports, but we were encouraged to be in everything we could because it might lead to scholarships for college. Guess what? They were exactly right. We earned scholarships for academics and activities helping with the financial burden. But the best part was that we loved school, learning, projects, and activities. My parents taught the pure joy of learning and that learning was our ticket to a successful life. They were very wise people.

They supported us in each project or activity that we participated in. They did not do it for us by any means, but they made sure that we had access to supplies and resources. Mom saved money and bought World Book Encyclopedias every time she could as a promotion from the local grocery store. Since we lived in the country, trips to the library were not frequent.

We all worked to help with college expenses but none of us siblings had any debt when we graduated. Mom and Dad's dreams were met by two of us achieving college degrees and honors. One sister learned that college was not for her but went on to be very successful in life.

I was blessed all along my academic journey with guides from 4-H leaders, to college advisors, and my advanced degree mentor, Dr. Kaye Sears. I enrolled in a master's program at the University of Central Oklahoma in Human Development. This choice was guided by my background in having a strong family; and wanting that for others. My dad started to suffer from Alzheimer's disease which is an awful thing. Watching my mom and dad struggle with this disease and its impact on the whole family made me desire to learn more about aging and adult development. Dr. Sears encouraged this pursuit by giving me the idea to conduct an intergenerational project for my creative and scholarly project for my master's program. This study and experience drove me to learn more. After taking some time to raise three small children and working as an adjunct professor at the University of Central Oklahoma, my mentor and life

> *Learn from the guides along the way, because I firmly believe that we can learn from anyone. It may be that after observing others, we choose to learn from them but select another path to our personal success.*

experiences guided me to enroll in a doctoral program with a specialization in gerontology. All the signs along the road pointed to this path. Take time along life's journey to make long-term goals for your career. Learn from the guides along the way, because I firmly believe that we can learn from anyone. It may be that after observing others, we choose to learn from them but select another path to our personal success. Hopefully, we will take the passion we observed in others and make it our own in whatever path we choose.

Be Open to New Ways to Learn

My personal journey has made me passionate about helping others learn about this process of aging. We are all aging each day, why not do it well? Traditional college age students sometimes have a difficult time understanding why they should learn as much as they can about aging successfully. Transformative learning experiences have unlocked the door for many students.

Service-learning experiences have provided the opportunity and motivation that students need to identify with the older population and their needs. Service learning is often used in our field of Family Life Education as a venue to help students understand concepts that they have learned through their textbooks and class discussions. It is also designed to benefit both the student and the recipient of the service activity. Many times, both the student and the recipient work together to benefit the community. An example of this philosophy is an intergenerational project that is in its second year with a local community partner near the campus. College students plan and implement this intergenerational program between four-year-old children and older adults. The project titled *Generations Learning Together*, meets bi-monthly throughout the semester at a local church that provides children from their childcare. The older adults are recruited in a variety of ways. This project was started as a research project through an on-campus grant fund. From data collected, we learned that the older adults, college students, and children all had improved attitudes about the other generations. Thus, enhancing awareness and improved understanding for our community. Another benefit of this project was that we were able to hire student workers through a couple of grants. The student workers/research assistants gained valuable experience about learning how to set up a research project, how to collect data, analyze data, write research proposals for conferences, present at conferences, and learn the basics of writing a professional journal article to report findings. Student research assistants attended a national conference, Association of Gerontology for Higher Education, with me and helped present the findings. They reported that this experience of presenting and attending the conference really helped their understanding of older adults. The students were thrilled to hear other researchers, that they had read their names in textbooks, present at the conference. From this they learned that they too could make a difference through research and caring. The students, as well as our interdisciplinary team, were all transformed by the intergenerational project.

Carefully planned service-learning experiences provide opportunities for students to integrate newfound classroom knowledge and theories into community service. These opportunities also provide valuable interaction with older adults. The students interact with the older adults through these events and start to identify with them as people just like them. Again, you never know who your guides for learning may be. Students are then encouraged to discuss their experiences in class. From these discussions, I have seen a huge growth in empathy and understanding about older adults. Comments shared from students have included: "They are just like us, some are shy, and some are not"; "I'm really impressed with how active Ms. X is!"; "Jimmie is so smart!"; and "They are so kind!". Another student commented, "I was a little afraid to go do my service-learning project. I didn't know what to expect exactly, but I had so much fun and was pleasantly surprised that I liked being there."

Growing up, I was not aware of policies and programs that affected older adults. Through personal experiences, I learned. As a result of this, I now teach a class titled *Policies and Programs for Older Adults.* There are so many helpful programs available for older adults. Students and society as a whole need to be more aware of these. Also, all of us need to be advocates for effective policies for all stages of life. As a result of this belief, students in this class serve as hosts/hostesses at Senior Day at the Capitol. This is a day where senior adults from across the state come and hear about what state agencies are advocating to improve programs and policies for older adults. The older adults are also given opportunities to visit with their legislators about their concerns. Students act as their guides through the capitol to find the legislators and also sit in the session about proposed policies and programs. This service-learning experience has really opened the eyes of students about what needs to be done through hearing compassionate, personal stories from the older adults. The older adults serve as teachers as they share their concerns. Many students state that they want to continue to serve in this role in subsequent years. Students are impressed with the knowledge and dedication that the older adults have to make a difference for themselves and those that they care about. This activity guides the students as they write their own proposed policy that they learn is needed through this experience for a major class assignment. Classroom discussions are much livelier after Senior Day at the Capitol!

This type of learning takes careful planning and organization, or students can become confused and frustrated by the experience. Laying the groundwork is very important with the discipline knowledge from the text and classroom activities. Follow up is also key to have critical reflection of the service-learning experience upon returning to class to debrief and to dialogue about the application of concepts. When students reach a level of transformation, they then can begin to integrate the overall experience with their personal view of working with older adults and what this process means for their own personal aging process. For some students, seeing themselves as aging is still difficult even after hands-on experiences with older adults. However, many times this does allow them more understanding of their loved ones that are aging. It also makes them curious to learn more about how they can help the older adults that

> *Through service learning and field experiences, students share that many beliefs that they held about diverse populations are simply not true and they start to question themselves, modifying their personal philosophy to be more open.*

they are in contact with.

Through service learning and field experiences, students share that many beliefs that they held about diverse populations are simply not true and they start to question themselves, modifying their personal philosophy to be more open. One student who served at the Alzheimer's Association through a field study project gained employment there. Field experiences give employers and students time to get to know each other and decide what is a good fit for both. Sometimes a student learns that the site is not a good fit for employment for them and that is valuable information as well. Contacts through the field experience/service learning can open other doors for employment.

Students become better prepared to serve on campus and off campus through transformative learning experiences. As a part of service learning and field experiences, students' awareness of community needs grows. They learn how to apply textbook knowledge to real life situations. Students develop skills in program planning, thus preparing them for identifying effective programs when they become professionals in the field. This type of learning opens up opportunities for students and faculty to work together with a common goal in mind; brainstorming together; and supporting each other to make a difference in this world. My students teach me so much from their perceptions of these opportunities. I'm hoping that they learn as much from me and the experiences as I learn from them.

Where is Your Learning Journey Taking You?

In reflection, the best advice I could give anyone is to take the time to evaluate each experience you have. Question yourself. Ask "what am I supposed to learn from this opportunity?" Accept every learning opportunity that you possibly can, such as conducting a research project or presenting at a conference. Get to know a variety of people along the way. Each person has something to offer. What skills can I take away from each person I meet? How can I apply this information to my life? Has this experience changed me in any way? Where do I go from here? What should be my next step? Evaluate, plan, and prepare for success. Watch the learning road signs and the mentors along your journey. Reflect and find your way to ongoing learning and life-time happiness. Enjoy the journey!

ANITA GLEE BERTRAM

Anita "Glee" Bertram, Ph.D., CFLE, is a professor in the Department of Human Environmental Sciences, University of Central Oklahoma. Glee has served as the principal investigator for several grants supporting programs or research concerning grandparents and presents findings yearly at conferences. Dr. Bertram teaches aging classes, coordinates many service-learning projects, and serves as the graduate intern coordinator.

Dr. Bertram co-sponsors the Central Council on Family Relations and is actively involved in the Oklahoma Council on Family Relations, National Council on Family Relations and the Association for Gerontology for Higher Education. During her twelve-year tenure, she has served on the Faculty Senate, Graduate Council, UCO Ambassador, Neely Award Selection Committee, CEPS Curriculum Committee, Tenure Committee, Grant Council Committee and CEPS Social Committee. Dr. Bertram has been honored to receive the Neely Excellence in Teaching Award in 2008, CEPS Vanderford Distinguished Teacher Award, Vanderford Engagement Award, and Student Advisor of the Year.

2

CHAPTER TWO

Wei R. Chen, Ph.D.

From a Factory Worker to a University Professor: A Transformative Journey of Learning and Teaching

My Education

From 1966 to 1976, China experienced an unprecedented cultural, political, and social storm—the Great Cultural Revolution. As a consequence, I had an unusual pre-college education. As far as I can remember, the schools were often closed, and studies were not encouraged. Every student seemed to have a predestined career: to become a member of the great society, either as a peasant, a factory worker, or a soldier.

From elementary school to high school, I spent more time practicing Chinese Kung Fu or playing Chinese bamboo flute than hitting the books. To most school kids, it was a wonderful time without the worries and anxieties of test taking or getting into colleges, which were either closed entirely or open only to a selected few. However, even under such circumstances, my desire to learn was always burning and never diminishing but buried deep inside of me.

I clearly recall that in elementary school, I read a fiction describing the irrigation system built by the Martians. It inspired me to learn more about Mars and ever since then, I have dreamt to visit the Martian-made canals. Well, the canals may not be there, but my dream has never died. More than 40 years later, I asked Milt Heflin, a former NASA flight director and an alumnus of the University of Central Oklahoma (UCO), to use his influence to get me a ticket to Mars, even just a one-way ticket. I was not entirely joking.

After high school, I was assigned a job working in a small factory as a metal sheet cutter to manufacture propane bottles. I spent more than two years in the factory. From time to time, I went to a nearby university to use their equipment for my job. I saw the students walking by with books in their hands and discussing things I could not comprehend. I was envious and wished to be one of them. Realizing that I might never attend college like those lucky few, my heart was bleeding, and I was in deep despair. However, I kept dreaming...dreaming that one day I would have the opportunity to continue my education in college.

I was blessed to have my dream quickly come true. The year 1976 marked the end of the Chinese Cultural Revolution. Universities and colleges in China reopened to everyone through fair competition. Previously ineligible high school graduates from the past ten years became eligible to take the joint college entrance exams to compete for a limited number of slots at universities and colleges across China. With an intense preparation in a few months, toiling on the factory floor during the day and burning night oils during the evening, I scored high on my college entrance exam and was admitted to Shandong University, majoring in theoretical high-energy particle physics, my first choice. I was indeed one of the luckiest students to get into the Class of 1977, among all the high school graduates from 1966 to 1977 in China. My college classmates consisted of factory workers, peasants, former solders, as well as young students who hadn't finished high school yet—an amazing collection of young men and women 15 to 35 years of age from all walks of life in China.

Needless to say, this first college class, after more than 10 years of turmoil, treasured the learning opportunity more than anything. A college life, to us, was definitely a privilege rather than a right. With a great desire to learn, I started my four-year intensive studies. Like a sponge, I was absorbing every drop of knowledge that I could get my hands on. I remember reading books using a flashlight under a thick blanket to defy the lights-out curfew after midnight. I spent most of my first summer vacation teaching myself calculus at home. Looking back, most people would say the students in Class of 1977 may have spent too much time studying and did not experience a normal college life, but for me, it was the best four years in my life. The solid academic background built upon the hard work during those four years was the result of my efforts to quench my thirst for knowledge and fulfill the dream I had as a previous factory worker.

During my last year at my alma mater, I received a scholarship to study in the United States. So, in 1982, I became a graduate student majoring in particle physics at the University of Oregon, facing more challenges than I anticipated, with little cultural background and limited English skills. As it did before, the desire to learn helped me struggle through all the cultural, social, and academic obstacles and challenges. Along the way, I married my wife and we had our first child. And with a Ph.D. degree in high-energy particle physics under my belt, I started my professional career in 1988.

My Education Career

Since my childhood, I have dreamt of being an educator because I believe teaching is the noblest profession. My interest in teaching also stemmed from my admiration and respect for my teachers. In fact, the most admired and respected historical figure in China, Confucius, was revered as the teacher of all teachers. I believe that everyone, particularly educators, has a heavy burden, since education not only affects the students today, but also has a long-lasting impact on society for many years to come. Another famous Chinese Philosopher, Guan Zhong (725-645 BC) once said, "If you plan for one year, plant rice. If you plan for ten years, plant trees. If you plan for 100 years, educate mankind." It best summarizes the importance of our profession. Indeed, my teaching philosophy has been largely based on traditional Chinese culture and Confucianism.

My innate strong desire to learn also urges me to share my knowledge with students. Hence, I started my professional career in education. After one year of college teaching and a short-term postdoctoral fellowship, I became one of the founding faculty members at the Oklahoma School of Science and Mathematics (OSSM), a residential school for gifted and talented students. I helped design the physics curriculum and taught young, bright students for ten years. It was during these ten years that I gained valuable experience and confidence in teaching. Particularly, I learned many ways in teaching and learning that were quite different from my upbringing and early education. It was also during this period that I began to develop my own teaching philosophy by integrating eastern and western teaching approaches.

It was also during my OSSM days that I shifted my research focus from theoretical high-energy particle physics to cancer research. While my love of particle physics and quest for understanding the sub-atomic world remain steadfast even today, my desire to reduce and relieve human pain and suffering has grown with age. In the early 1990s, I joined a research group at the University of Oklahoma Health Sciences Center, just in time to initiate a project using lasers for cancer treatment with my collaborators. Within a few years, our team developed laser immunotherapy, a unique combination of local laser irradiation and local immunostimulation using a novel compound, glycated chitosan. More than 20 years later, with seven U.S. patents and over 100 peer-reviewed articles, laser immunotherapy has been developed from a simple concept, to a bench-top research project, to clinical trials. In the treatment of late-stage, metastatic melanoma and breast cancer patients, laser immunotherapy has shown promising outcomes. This drastic change in my research focus reflected my never-ending desire to learn and my passion to serve people. I often use this particular experience in my teaching to remind my students that change can be good and to inspire students to embrace changes in life.

In 1999, I moved to the University of Central Oklahoma (UCO), opening a new chapter in my professional career. In addition to my continued efforts in cancer research and teaching classes at different levels, my interest in interdisciplinary education and research also grew, since I recognized that advancements in science and technology have broken down all boundaries of different fields. In 2000, I took the leadership role in developing the Biomedical Engineering (BME) undergraduate degree program. I designed the BME curriculum and developed and taught the new BME classes. Integrating biological and physical sciences, mathematics, and engineering, UCO established the first BME undergraduate degree program in the state of Oklahoma.

To further enhance collaborations between faculty and students in different fields, I established the Center for Interdisciplinary Biomedical Education and Research (CIBER). CIBER members are from six different departments and two different colleges at UCO. With regular meetings and close interactions, the faculty and students share laboratories, equipment, and, above all, ideas leading to joint research grant proposals and joint publications. The annual CIBER Symposium, showcasing student research, started in 2014. The concept of interdisciplinary education and research exemplified by CIBER and other centers led to UCO's new 57,000 square feet Donald Betz STEM Research and Learning Center in 2018.

Teaching is indeed a rewarding career for me. In 2008, I was selected as the US Professor of the Year by the Council for Advancement and Support of Education and the Carnegie Foundation for the Advancement of Teaching. In 2011, I received the Medal of Excellence in Teaching Award from

Above all, the best reward has been seeing my students grow in their own knowledge and passion to learn.

the Oklahoma Foundation for Excellence. In 2012, I was presented with the Educator Award by the International Society of Optics and Photonics. I attribute these achievements to the support of my students and colleagues, as well as to my desire to learn and my passion to teach. Above all, the best reward has been seeing my students grow in their own knowledge and passion to learn.

My Education Philosophy

Although my pre-college education was scattered and irregular, and my college education was heavily focused on physics, Chinese culture—particularly the teachings of Confucius—still had a significant impact on my professional life. While learning how to adapt to a new life in the U.S., I also learned how to integrate the teaching and learning philosophies of different cultures. During my educational career of over 30 years, I have adopted a three-part, student-centered, transformative learning strategy, which is deeply rooted in Chinese culture—a part of my ethnic heritage—and in the teaching philosophies of Confucius.

The first is individual-based learning according to a student's background, knowledge, and skills, which is based on the philosophy of Confucius: "Teach according to the student's ability." I carry this out especially in my research lab, where I have students coming from all different experience levels. Based on each student's background and interests, I design different projects for them. Some undergraduate students are able to design their own projects and carry out independent experiments, reporting their findings in refereed publications. In other cases, I work with students every step of the way, helping them master basic laboratory skills and move on to conduct research. I also serve as a mentor and advisor for students in independent studies, internships, and summer projects, with individually designed projects. My objective is to help students learn and reach their highest potential.

> *During my educational career of over 30 years, I have adopted a three-part, student-centered, transformative learning strategy, which is deeply rooted in Chinese culture—a part of my ethnic heritage—and in the teaching philosophies of Confucius.*

The second part of my strategy applies an inquiry-based learning process that incorporates experiential learning. Confucius once said, "I hear and I forget. I see and I remember. I do and I understand." I often design and assign projects to students requiring experiments or simulations to acquire knowledge, either independently or with teamwork. I believe that this hands-on experience gives my students a competitive edge in their future professional careers and graduate education. I emphasize in my teaching that the most important aspect of learning is the process of acquiring knowledge, not just knowledge itself. "Doing" is the best way to learn. Experiential learning is the key to success.

The third part of the strategy is an interdisciplinary approach in learning to ensure students' competitiveness in today's global economy. My efforts at UCO in developing a medical physics program, establishing a biomedical engineering program, as well as creating CIBER, reflect my desire to pursue interdisciplinary education and research. I also take an interdisciplinary approach in my research on cancer treatment. In my lab, students work on all components of laser immunotherapy, a novel treatment method involving different fields, such as laser physics, engineering designs, mathematical simulations, biology, and chemistry. Projects include laser delivery system design, temperature determination, drug administration, immunological assays, as well as animal treatment and observations. With my students working in different disciplines and working together as a team, they gain a better understanding of the project and master skills in different fields.

Several larger themes also embedded in my teaching. I emphasize to my students that college is the place where they learn how to think and develop their methods of approaching real-life problems. I convey the message that the only constant in the real world is "change." I often challenge them with open-ended questions that reflect real-world challenges. For example, I introduce students to the status of cancer and development of treatment methods so that they can consider ways to tackle similar problems.

Also important to a student's growth is service learning. I constantly try to infuse the notion that the purpose of learning is to serve people and to contribute to society, not merely to enrich oneself. I challenge my students to save or change at least one person's life in their career. My dream is to have my students come to me one day and tell me they did just that.

I encourage students to develop passion and compassion in their education and training. If they do not find passion for their current career, I encourage them to embrace change. I often use my career change as an example. At age 33, after 15 years of education and research experience in high-energy physics, I started cancer research. I have been richly rewarded by the change in my career path.

Summary

After working in the classroom for more than 30 years, I still enjoy teaching. It is interesting to note that the class I have enjoyed teaching most is Quantum Mechanics, part of my first love in my professional life. I maintain a sizable research lab with a large group of undergraduate students, graduate students, postdoctoral fellows, and visiting scholars. I still strive to achieve my highest potential in all areas of academic life: teaching, scholarship, and service.

Today, we are facing crises in many areas, particularly in education. At the same time, we are also provided with unprecedented opportunities. In Chinese, "crisis" is composed of two characters: "danger" and "opportunity." Indeed, it falls on the shoulders of our educators to face this danger and to seize the opportunity to educate our students for many generations to come.

The journey from a factory worker to a university professor is continuing and my desire to learn and teach never withers. I am continuously transformed with my students.

WEI R. CHEN

Wei R. Chen, Ph.D. (University of Oregon) serves as Professor of Biomedical Engineering and Dean of the College of Mathematics and Science, at the University of Central Oklahoma. He is the co-inventor of laser immunotherapy for metastatic cancers—which has been used in initial clinical trials for late-stage, metastatic melanoma and breast cancer patients with promising outcomes. He is also the inventor of an immunologically modified carbon nanotube used in photoimmunotherapy for cancers. He has published more than 150 peer-reviewed articles and more than 160 conference proceeding papers. He has been awarded 9 U.S. patents and several international patents. He has received more than $7 million for research and education from federal and state agencies, as well as from private foundations and industrial sponsors. He was selected as a SPIE (International Society for Optics and Photonics) Fellow in 2007 and the U.S. Professor of the Year in 2008. In 2009, Chen received the Neely Excellence in Teaching award.

3 CHAPTER THREE
Jeanetta D. Sims, Ph.D.

Rhythm, Movement, and Patterns: How a Love of Dance Stimulated a Love of Learning

Growth requires movement
Leaving welcome, comfortable space
To usher in uncertainty
For something new to take its place.

> *Trial* requires effort
> Casting hope against a chance
> At realized opportunity
> Make a choice to move and dance.

Learning requires both
Constant *growth* through *trial*
To make imperfect attempts
That risk discomfort to reveal one's style.

> Dare to grow.
> Dare to try.
> Dare to learn.
> **Dare to dance.**

> ~ Jeanetta D. Sims

Earliest reflections of my learning begin in dance classes at Gloria's School of Dance in a rural Oklahoma town. At age 4 as an African American preschooler, I began lessons in tap, jazz, and ballet in a studio full of all White people except for me, the lone brown-skinned Black girl. I excelled and caught on quickly, which prompted my teacher to move me up a class grade. Through dance, I realized that I had the capacity to learn. I could challenge my mind with the retention of a series of steps, and I could emulate exceptional instruction whether in-person or on a recorded VHS tape. Once I had captured the essentials of every genre, I was ready to tackle sophisticated combinations. Each sequence was a pattern of movement, and I came to appreciate how readily my mind was equipped to recognize the patterns.

Seeing the patterns in commonalities or in structure across multiple disciplines has been a key catalyst for my academic career success, which has been quite interdisciplinary. Today, my teaching, research, service, and administrative load along with undergraduate student research engagement has a keen sense of rhythm and movement much like dance. I have used the cognitive capability of generating patterns to guide and organize each facet of my work as well as to learn from the work of others. These simple aspects of dance coupled with creativity have been pervasive in my personal story of transformation. This brief essay offers a summary of personal reflections on learning that began from dancing in my youth. I offer instructive insights and cautions for learners of all ages, and, in particular, encouragement to teachers and learners of color.

Dance, Dance, Dance, and Lessons Along the Way

The lessons learned from growing up with dance are numerous. From time steps and jazz hands to pliés and stretching, I have continued the joy of dance into adulthood. This section offers some of my most memorable moments of dance. Throughout the reflections, I offer lessons and share the links to learning.

I was going to be a dancer. Like Debbie Allen's choreography and Gregory Hines' tapping techniques, I was going to be *smooth*, have impact, and capture the imagination. And, I didn't mind the work of movement. Along with watching the weekly television show, *Fame*, as if it were a once-in-a-lifetime occurrence, I planned activities around viewing the Academy Awards or Tony Awards where top dancers performed a showcase of Debbie Allen's work. These were brief dance minutes of an hour's-long award show interspersed between announcements of award winners. If I were lucky, Debbie Allen would perform herself. Most people watched the awards shows to learn the winners; I watched the awards shows strictly for glimpses of dance.

Pay attention. You will have glimpses of outstanding educational examples much as I did with dance choreographers. Acknowledge them. Follow them, particularly when their values align with a desire to invest in someone else's potential. The investment could be in you. In high school, DeAnn Pence, my home economics teacher, was responsible for giving me multiple opportunities to grow and an early educational example to emulate. From high school speech competitions and local awards to statewide leadership positions and an international summer exchange to Japan, I benefited from Pencie Poo's (as I always affectionately called her) investment and full commitment to her students. In my undergraduate, master's and doctoral programs, the late Michael Pfau and a host of other faculty offered excellent examples of mentorship, advocacy, and encouragement. This group of educators withheld no opportunities from me and were incredibly persuasive in offering reasons for why I, as a first-generation college student, should "jump" from the ledge and into the next learning opportunity. Their mentorship and treatment of me provided the safety net for my learning. Great inspiring examples exist worth emulating, whether they reside in the context of dance or education. Be alert to look for them since they likely already surround you.

Eventually in my early to mid-teens, I would attend Johnny Tremaine dance conventions in Dallas, Texas, where a hotel ballroom full of dancers would learn the full choreography for an entire song in less than an hour. At this quick pace, attendees learned multiple routines to popular songs over the course of a full Saturday of dance. I spent dance convention days standing shoulder to shoulder next to mostly strangers who all shared a love of dance. My aim of convention attendance was not winning a competition or standing out above other dancers; instead, the purpose was perfecting my own movement while learning under someone else's instruction.

Be careful. Avoid roadblocks that prevent you from furthering your learning. If you are like me as a dancer, you will have distractions in your educational efforts that seek to pull you away from your primary purpose, which is furthering your own learning or improving your own movement. These distractions can include any of the following:

- seeking the trophy (e.g., a learner desiring an award or recognition);
- complaining about the dance instructor (e.g., the learner claiming to have a horrible teacher);
- attempting to have the perfect dance (e.g., the learner working exclusively to get the "right" grade);
- looking at the movement of other dancers (e.g., the learner comparing self to other learners); and,
- obsessing about having the right tights or stage for the performance (e.g., the learner waiting for the right tools, equipment, or time to further their learning).

While many of these are worthy aims or outcomes, we often allow them to undermine our efforts and permit them to provide us with what we perceive to be justifiable excuses to delay or ignore seizing learning opportunities. However, if the personal aim is to improve our own movement, the caution here is to cut out the excuses and just dance. Follow your curiosity and learn for the pure joy of learning.

As a troupe, our dance class competed across genres in dance competitions to win trophies and raise the reputation of our small-town studio. I spent practices learning from and working to move in concert with others who did not look like me. It was fun, and we enjoyed much success. Then, my dance teacher asked me to compete with a tap solo that required one-on-one studio training sessions. I was honored and eager to continue learning. When the first competition came, I experienced the typical nervous backstage jitters prior to performing. The routine began smoothly with showmanship and rhythmic taps on beat. And, then I

> *Give yourself permission to engage constantly in imperfect trials; risk the perfect outcome to gain new learning experiences.*

froze. Like a deer in headlights, I stood on stage without the slightest recollection of my next move. As trained, I stumbled through the routine and made up moves for a portion of the performance, before returning to my rehearsed movement to reach the end of the music. Yet, the solo performance in no way resembled what I had anticipated or what I thought I had perfected. From my perspective, the performance was disastrous! People lose their train of thought all the time. But, how could I have lost it in the middle of my performance? And, why the failure in my first-ever solo competition? I was crushed.

Expect failure. Put more gently, anticipate missing the mark from time to time. Unlike my first solo competition from years ago, today, imperfect trials at learning have become my friends; they permit me to practice, to explore, and to inquire without the fear of getting it wrong. Learners need space to engage in trials and to test out ideas. In future dance and performance attempts, I would go on to earn awards in solo and individual competitions where I would risk the fear of freezing up again for another shot at growth. In each experience, I learned more about myself and about how best to prepare my mind for upcoming opportunities. Give yourself permission to engage constantly in imperfect trials; risk the perfect outcome to gain new learning experiences.

The Step, Ball Change of My Transformation in Learning and Teaching

Fast forward more than 40 years from my first dance class and you will still find me learning and interested in patterns. The youthful exuberance of rewinding VHS tapes to learn moves from Gregory Hines, Debbie Allen, and Janet Jackson still exists, though, with a different type of movement. Today's movement is now a fascination with learning from great educators, excellent teachers, and those across all industries who lead with authenticity. And, I must admit that sometimes, I still dance or bounce to my favorite music while working in higher education. It has become my way of finding my own rhythm and challenging what I thought I knew about teaching and learning. In more ways than I can articulate, my early years in dance have affected my own personal teaching and learning transformation. This section discusses how these insights and experiences have transformed my teaching and learning.

I reference my early experiences of often being the only person of color in the dance studio, because perceptions and misperceptions of race have often confounded my learning both in dance and in education. In dance, I learned people expected me to have rhythm as they interacted with me while drawing from racial stereotypes. Yes, difference matters, and many stories from my interactions exist to support this assertion.

Yet, my most salient experience of racial stereotypes occurred when I mentioned interest in a college major of psychology to a school official. "You'll need to get a master's degree to do that. And, you're going to have a family and end up with babies," he said. Pause. Regardless of the intent of his comments or instruction, I heard his remarks as a put down and as the operationalization of racial and gender stereotypes for Black girls like me. It appeared his prevailing schemas were that (1) I would become pregnant, and (2) that my pregnancy would curtail any academic and professional pursuits. How does one dance as a person of color when others misrepresent or cannot identify with one's aspirations? Find your own movement and your own style anyway, while expecting to face opposition.

Years later, I returned to the same school as a professor to guest speak at an awards banquet. Upon seeing me, another school official encouraged me to send my résumé to the man who had made the above comments. I was stunned. For years, I had no idea anyone else besides me had heard his remarks. While I could have sent a lengthy document that chronicled my educational degrees, positions held, presentations, publications, and honors as a sort of in-your-face gesture, I never did. It was never about him anyway; instead, I have learned that my Ph.D. pursuit and educational interests have always been about my own movement, which to me has meant demonstrating a personal willingness to sacrifice, try, learn, and grow while helping others along the way.

For all learners and, in particular, for learners with salient African American or female identities, my presence as a fellow learner, researcher, professor, and dean matters.

Given my experiences as an African American, female, scholar mom, I understand that I may be the only African American teacher or research mentor my students and research assistants have ever had. For all learners and, in particular, for learners with salient African American or female identities, my presence as a fellow learner, researcher, professor, and dean matters. This is especially true if I remain a learner who is willing to share challenges experienced while finding her own movement;[1] this openness may inspire others to do so as well.

Along with demonstrating my own learning through leading by example, I am mindful of the need to encourage reciprocal learning and create opportunities for collaboration in my teaching and research. Through collaborative teaching, I have transformed my classrooms to become "co-created spaces of learning,"[2] where students shape the design of the course syllabus. In the first few weeks of class, learners dictate the direction of the course. In my program of research, which has a focus on persuasion and influence, strategic communication, marketing, and workforce diversity, student learning is at the forefront. Now in its 12th year, Diverse Student Scholars[3] (see the program website: www.diversestudentscholars.com), which is an interdisciplinary program of student research engagement, provides students with in- and out-of-class opportunities to learn and interact through research engagement.

Along with classroom shifts and a more inclusive program of research toward collaboration, I have transformed my teaching and mentoring in more specific, intentional ways to accommodate diverse learners. From providing per diem in advance for group conference presentation travel and entertaining questions on a range of topics related to professional attire, how to pack for air travel, and how to navigate work-life balance, I have been accessible to diverse learners and learners of color as they undergo their own learning journeys. My biggest transformation from teaching and mentoring learners of color is not that *they must* do or be something different; instead, I understand that *I must.* Very often, I *must* take action or learn more to improve my teaching and mentorship. For learners with a lower socio-economic status, I have secured resources and explained how they can continue to take advantage of funded opportunities without having to bear any additional costs from the dance of academic research engagement. For learners who differ on other diversity dimensions (e.g., whether religious, race, sexual orientation, 1st generation student status, ability, etc.), I listen for concerns and encourage them as research assistants to keep a list of questions that pop up for them. They are encouraged to pose questions from their list during the next weekly face-to-face meeting. This ensures we have an ongoing method built into our routine work for discussing concerns or clarifying misconceptions.

Some learners across various diversity dimensions are simply ready to perform and only require a stage and an opportunity. However, others need more one-on-one studio lessons or a different type of instruction. As a teacher and research faculty mentor, I have learned it is my responsibility to invest in the learner's potential, to discover the learner's desires, and to facilitate movement toward our learning objectives. While learners personalize their own journeys, teachers facilitate and advocate for students' learning.

The Encore as Additional Insights for Movement

Surround yourself with people who are willing to support your leap. At some point, the dancer who leaps has to leave the ground. In other words, she must be willing to momentarily disregard occupying the existing space while having confidence in a landing that leads to the next series of steps. Therefore, yes, the dancer leaps. However, the dancer is not *alone* in the leaping, even if it is a solo performance. Supporting the performance and the dancer are individuals who make the performance possible—a choreographer, costume designer, lighting director, sound technician and a host of others. Rarely, if ever, do dancers cue their own music as they stand on stage for the performance. So, give yourself room to leap, and though you may work hard alone to perfect your movement and series of next steps, understand the value and importance of having a team of people to support, mentor, and advocate for you.

Be flexible and willing to take calculated risks in your learning before you leap. Have you ever attempted to tap dance on a slick floor? I certainly have, and the silvery metal taps landing on the shiny surface severely limited my ability to leap, do wings (this is a tap dance move), and remain standing. The experience gave me a newfound appreciation for being adaptive, while examining the floor, foundation, and other factors prior to any movement. Often, it appears as if people just "dive" right into learning or into pursuing their professional aspirations. Perhaps, some who do this find success. However, many, many more of the people that I admire considered their surroundings and intentionally moved about with context in mind. Some completed temporary internships so they could learn more about a particular industry. Others took lower paying positions for an opportunity to work with a supervisor, team, or company that they admired. In addition, many saved to afford study tours or trips abroad in an effort to expand their exposure to teaching and learning on a global scale. Each were flexible and their calculated risk paid off with greater learning and a broader network of support for their next leap. First, understand the nature of the foundation, climate, and culture in which you are seeking to perform, and then dive right in.

You do not have to "know" how to dance or seek others' confirmation to find your own movement. A misguided notion of dancing and learning is that engaging in both requires someone else's approval. They simply do not. Remember, you are seeking to advance your own and not someone else's movement. Thus, you are responsible for your own movement and your own learning. And, you should permit no one to entrap you by keeping you ignorant (unlearned) and by preventing your learning.

Enslavement through ignorance is entrapment. Most of us, if we are honest, who began our careers as educators must admit to knowing very little when we first began. We were simply curious and willing to risk the personal pursuit of finding out more about our curiosity. If you are waiting to know everything before learning, you will be greatly disappointed to find yourself in the same space with little to no movement. Instead, trust the 6-month-old girl who bounces and grins to music while bobbing her head up and down, and remember the example of the jamming, 75-year-old man who finds himself in the dance cam lens during a baseball game. You can wiggle, shake, or nod to the beat of your favorite song whenever you want. Similarly, learning begins whenever you are ready; you simply seek to find your own movement. You can perfect your personal dance as you go, or it can stay under construction while you continue to test out your favorite moves. You need not *know* everything to get started. Just begin.

The Final Bow

This essay provides a rare opportunity to reflect and write on my personal learning journey. The narrative offers insights gleaned through dance and associated connections or cautions for learners. Additionally, I provide evidence of my transformation and greater sense of mindfulness in representing learners of color and in encouraging all diverse learners. My hope is for you, the reader, to have a greater appreciation for your own movement and to develop your own style of dance as a lifelong learner.

JEANETTA D. SIMS

Jeanetta D. Sims, Ph.D., is dean of the Jackson College of Graduate Studies and a tenured professor in the College of Business department of marketing at the University of Central Oklahoma. Her program of research includes strategic communication, workforce diversity, and persuasion and social influence. She teaches courses in marketing and communication and is accredited in public relations (APR). She founded and cultivated a robust, interdisciplinary, student research program in 2007 called Diverse Student Scholars as her personal contribution to the Academy. Embedded research mentorship is a key feature of her teaching strategy and co-curricular student engagement. Dr. Sims has received top paper awards for her research in nine of the last 13 years, which includes recognition in every discipline associated with her teaching. Along with receiving the Neely Excellence in Teaching Award in her 2nd year of teaching in 2009, she has received teaching awards from the Marketing Management Association and Oklahoma Christian University.

CHAPTER FOUR

Gladys Lewis, Ph.D.

The Inside/Outside Sources for Learning and Teaching

L earning travels in the double harness of inside/outside strengths that predisposes a teaching paradigm. The interior learning motivation originates with individual curiosity that prompts the desire to learn answers to questions. The exterior part of the tandem results when a person or situation provides answers to those questions. When the two learning sources produce an interaction, learning occurs. The formula repeats until accrued learning reaches a level to render the learner a teacher for another person with questions to be answered. This predictable action between a learner and a teacher continues through life to be the manner in which learning and teaching occur. At any time, a person may be the searcher or the teacher. Two elements with a result support the process; the searcher must respond to spontaneous urges that create the knowledge quest and a teacher must be available to provide information to satisfy the quest. The result shapes a transformative experience as each stage of life involves a new culture of learning and teaching to form an encompassing embrace of knowledge that vibrates in our cells.

Inside/Outside Learning and Teaching in Childhood

Inside/Outside Learning and Teaching occurred for me in early childhood and shaped basic lifelong learning patterns. My Aunt Hazel, thirteen years older than I, took me—always curious and questioning—as her special project. She taught me to read and write long before I entered school. In the farm community where I grew up, children started to school in the summer, then had a fall recess when they helped with harvest. In June, barely five, I started to first grade because we had no kindergarten in my rural consolidated school. Grades one through six were taught two grades to a room by one teacher. Two unmarried sisters who lived in an apartment above the garage of the general store at the crossroads of the school's location were known as Miss First-Second Grade Lollar and Miss Third-Fourth Grade Lollar. Mrs. Hunt taught the fifth and sixth grades. The first six years of my educational life were shaped by those three women. Like goddesses on Olympus, they answered my questions. Best of all, they kept books in their rooms that they loaned me, a practice I enacted with my students. I read *Beowulf* and *Song of Roland*, oldest English and French literature, which provided my beginning love for Anglo-Saxon and Medieval literature. The texts added to my later fascination with the *Camino de Santiago de Compostela*, the medieval pilgrim route beginning with the pass leading through the mountains where the Battle of Roncevaux in 778 was fought, the site for *Song of Roland*. With the information from my early classrooms, I became my own teacher. An antique horse-drawn road grader on the farm with a huge steering wheel became a ship's rudder when the grader metamorphosed into a ship, and I sailed the world in it, capturing real and imagined adventures from the books I read. The haystack, a dozen bales high, became an observatory where I tested wind currents and wondered how clouds were made. I validated the updraft of a dirt oven made with a post-hole digger in a creek bank to bake a potato in a closed fire. The magic of knowing created the incumbent constraint to teach. My doll and my little sister became my students and, toy six-shooter strapped to my waist (I *was* a farm child), I fervently shared that which I knew. As Margaret O'Brien ("Tootie") in *Meet Me in St. Louis* buried her dolls, we buried Molly Ann, time-worn by education. Like other outgrown items in passing through a learning culture, I discarded my gun. To this day, my sister is an avid reader.

Transformative Takeaway: Inside/Outside Learning and Teaching occurs in early childhood and shapes basic learning patterns.

Inside/Outside Learning and Teaching in Adolescence

Inside/Outside Learning and Teaching can follow in age appropriate life events to shape transformative life attitudes. Late in my sixth grade, my family moved to Oklahoma City. In addition to the cultural shift from a rural to an urban setting, I encountered a different educational structure. From my teachers came a growing sophistication of information to be learned and explored. At the deeper level of interaction, however, the process I had known with Aunt Hazel, the Misses Lollar, and Mrs. Hunt remained unchanged: learner>teacher> transformation. I acquired many ancillary skills and information. Quickly, I understood the value of the arts, the expanding role of sports, competitions, scholastic achievement, and recognition. As a senior, I wrote a counterview of Lady McBeth in an essay, which my English teacher submitted to a city-wide contest, and I won! With five dollars as prize, my picture was printed on the front page of the school paper with the headline, "Sherman Wins Bard Contest." I was hooked, not by receiving money, but by seeing my words and name in print. Latin study brought awareness of the bedrock contribution of Latin to our linguistic and professional languages. The inter-relationships of the disciplines I met reflected to my mind-sponge the mutual interdependence of all knowledge. Peers taught me that social skills related to learning. Because I made good grades, my classmates frequently asked me for help. Learning is respected; teaching is welcomed. Required diplomatic skill arrived in assimilating the correct manner with the right attitude in offering help. Gender boundaries were more fixed than they are now. In a burst of political adventuring, I ran for student council president. A female teacher in coaching on political strategy, said to my male opponent, "Act bored, like she is no competition," and to me, she said, "Just be sweet." I lost the election, but dropped the sweetness, ran again the next semester, and won. This was not my first introduction to gender disparities. One Christmas while we lived on the farm, the school program was scheduled on a night that turned cold with stormy rain. We went in our horse-drawn wagon. Upon arrival, I was asked by the program director to learn several parts of children who were not present. As we were about to go on stage, she said to me, "Oh, wait. A boy has to be first." I understood, like the time I was Betsy Ross with her flag following George Washington and Abraham Lincoln. With time, adherence to learning, and patience, I had my turns at being first on the stage, hosting open house surprises.

Transformative Takeaway: Inside/Outside Learning and Teaching can follow in age appropriate life events to shape transformative life attitudes.

Inside/Outside Learning and Teaching in Nursing School

Inside/Outside Learning and Teaching can predispose one to diversity and tolerant thinking when confronted by radically different learning environments. I graduated from high school in pre-student loan days. My family did not have college funds. I decided to attend a three-year nursing school to become a registered nurse under the older apprentice-style educational system when the student paid a nominal fee for classes in a closed environment and supplemented that fee with work on the wards commensurate with the learning level. I became a nurse in order to have a profession and a way to support myself while I went on to university study, my determined goal. The learning culture came from different kinds of textbooks and from observing and validating evidence for them from patients. Learning rewards resulted with understanding the factual information from instructors, testing what I learned from exchanges with patients, and teaching that took place with my instructions to patients. My ability to listen with all my senses responding to my fascination with the human body, appreciating the reliability of the body to tell the truth, and trusting the patient as a conveyor of bodily information provided learning. With basic healthcare information, I gained common-sense approaches to running a healthcare facility and gained nursing procedures in the most efficient, economical manner possible, priceless knowledge for my decade of service in a mission hospital in South America. Attuned to my learning model in my three-year Catholic nursing school, I absorbed the value of growth inside another religious system different from mine which engendered respect for all faiths in all cultures as I climbed their walls of mystery.

> *My ability to listen with all my senses responding to my fascination with the human body, appreciating the reliability of the body to tell the truth, and trusting the patient as a conveyor of bodily information provided learning.*

Transformative Takeaway: Inside/Outside Learning and Teaching can predispose one to diversity and tolerant thinking when confronted by radically different learning environments.

Inside/Outside Learning and Teaching in University Study

University study takes the inside to the outside for affirmation in the educational process. With the move into university study, new disciplines required mastery. Though I loved my combined role as liberal arts student and campus nurse with scientific knowledge, joy marinated the study in the humanities and literature, my first love. The social and intellectual environment brought different learning formats. My nursing school inside questions came from information presented in class lectures and independent functioning in the wards. Teachers had hierarchical positions in some settings, but also side-by-side presence in others. In the university, the emphasis rested more upon the classroom information. Reading assignments, research, and independent study set me free to answer my own inside questions. I provided findings to professors whose outside assistance came in responses to my work which increased self-confidence and trust of personal findings in repeating tides of acquisition.

Transformative Takeaway: University study takes the inside to the outside for affirmation in the educational process.

Inside/Outside Learning and Teaching in Mission Service

Adjustment to radical cultural shifts, at times accompanied by the unexpected, is aided by the Inside/Outside learning paradigm, individual interests, and a sense of humor. I met and married my surgeon husband when he was a senior medical student and I was a year from having the coveted bachelor's degree. We both were starry-eyed do-gooders from early childhood. With the completion of formal education and our two small children, we journeyed to the Baptist Hospital in Asuncion, Paraguay, to offer our service. We traveled by riverboat 1,500 miles from Buenos Aires, Argentina, to Paraguay on the Parana/Paraguay River system when the area had experienced a record dry summer and fall. Because the river level was not high enough to support landing at the port, we had to trans-board mid-river and land on the riverbank at Asuncion in our *chata*, the name for both the barge and a bedpan, somewhat symbolic we thought. Memories of learning come from the trans-boarding of our boxes and hospital supplies. After a year in language school in Costa Rica, I arrived with impeccable language skills only to learn that Spanish was a second language to Guarani-speaking-Paraguayans as it was to me. And the male-first hierarchy was culturally entrenched. I also learned of Paraguayan fascination with blond, blue-eyed children as I watched men pitching my two-year-old son, David, back and forth between the barge and the boat. I called my gregarious husband, deep in jovial conversation with fellow passengers, to rescue our son. The men paid me no attention as they and David squealed with laughter at the game. During our receptions at the hospital, humor provided my resistance mode. With great flourishes, the hospital pharmacist introduced my husband, gave him a hug, *un abraso*, and turned back to the crowd. On impulse, I asked, "*No hay abraso para mi* (There is no hug for me?)" The crowd burst into laughter. The hug came, followed by many others. With character revealed in humor, my responses were always reciprocated. Moreover, writing opportunities arrived with the healthcare. I wrote a Spanish text for nursing ethics for the nursing school and headed a newsletter for the hospital and employees, an anticipated and enjoyed offering through friendship's hands.

Transformative Takeaway: Adjustment to radical cultural shifts, at times accompanied by the unexpected, is aided by the Inside/Outside learning paradigm, individual interests, and a sense of humor.

Inside/Outside Learning and Teaching in Graduate Study

Inside/Outside patterns become more integrative and reciprocal when facing new settings. When the youngest of my four children entered high school, I decided to return to graduate study. I earned a Master of Arts degree in English/Creative Writing and continued in a Doctor of Philosophy program. Another new social, cultural, and intellectual environment took over my life. Although graduate study became the most challenging of my experiences, it also provided one of my happiest eras with countless hours spent in study. I learned from esteemed professors how to relate to students with dignity and to be welcomed as colleagues in the discipline. With my peers, I formed learning groups to be teachers to each other, following the North Star of my learning pattern.

> *Being a faculty member in the classroom posed different positions...While I treasured my status, I never flouted nor violated; I had learned productive interactions from cherished professors who formed my understanding of the teaching and learning enterprise as a faculty member.*

Transformative Takeaway: Inside/Outside patterns become more integrative and reciprocal when facing new settings.

Inside/Outside Learning and Teaching as a Faculty Member

The mutual interaction of the inside/outside paradigm blends both areas. When I became a faculty member at the University of Central Oklahoma, I encountered a new structure where I was located at the top of the learning hierarchy. Being a faculty member in the classroom posed different positions. I was leader and authority in the class organization. While I treasured my status, I never flouted nor violated; I had learned productive interactions from cherished professors who formed my understanding of the teaching and learning enterprise as a faculty member. I loved my students, sincerely, and loved my job. My students loved me in return. They stay in touch, want me to know about their lives, and re-connect when they are in town. Our model transforms them and me and welcomes the intimacy of shared minds. No longer billed for ignorance, their success empowers me and them.

Transformative Takeaway: The mutual interaction of the inside/outside paradigm blends both areas.

Inside/Outside Learning and Teaching in Retirement

Happiness comes with the transformative results of merging and molding in the process of inside/outside learning, teaching, and remaining curious. In retirement, the model still directs me. Always curious, I commend that characteristic to my children and grandchildren as the beginning of learning. I love to work. Currently, I am both an editor for Baylor University Press and personal editor for five authors. I don't physically meet the writers whom I serve, but enduring friendships develop from our online hours together. When minds connect, I learn, they learn, and a book results. The same paradigm of inside/outside interaction remains for me in editing as it has in all teaching and learning first met when I was five. My ten-year-old grandson, Parker, said recently during a sleepover weekend with me, "GG, retirement must be great. You have that chocolate, the popcorn, and all you have to do is take the check to the bank." I replied, "Like you, Parker, darlin', I am curious and ask questions to learn about life and enjoy it. The check has been going to the bank for years."

Transformative Takeaway: Happiness comes with the transformative results of merging and molding in the process of inside/outside learning, teaching, and curiosity.

GLADYS LEWIS

Gladys Sherman Lewis, R.N., A.B., M.A., Ph.D., native Oklahoman, spent a year in San Jose, Costa Rica, in the Spanish Language School (*La Escuela de Idiomas*) with her surgeon husband, Wilbur, learning Spanish in preparation for their decade of service at the Baptist Hospital in Asuncion, Paraguay. With their return to the United States, she participated in many levels of denominational life as a writer, speaker, and member of various boards. In the 1980s, she returned to graduate study in literature. Her Ph.D. work at Oklahoma State University focused on British and American literature. She joined the faculty of the University of Central Oklahoma in 1991 and remained there twenty-two years until her retirement in 2013. Treasured honors were the College of Liberal Arts' Lifetime Achievement Award, the University of Central Oklahoma's Neely Excellence in Teaching award in 2012, and the Oklahoma 2012 Regional University Excellence in Teaching Award.

5 CHAPTER FIVE

John F. Barthell, Ph.D.

A Comfort with Uncertainty

I grew up in the Bighorn Basin of Wyoming in and around a community of less than 5,000 people, situated midway between Yellowstone Park and the Bighorn Mountains. I assume my parents moved us to that remote location not only because they found jobs there but because they also thought it would be a great place to live. They were right about that and most of my formative experiences can be tied to that place and the people I met and became acquainted with while living there. I learned my work ethic through long hours of pulling weeds from pinto bean fields among thousands of acres of rich but irrigated farmland in the Basin during those days. Between the mentorship of farmers and my parents, the value of being up early and ending one's workday late developed as a principle that has not strayed from my current values.

What inspired me in those days was an abiding curiosity about Nature and what made living organisms "tick." I was relentless as a child in trying to pursue anything that I could in this vein, including rearing mourning cloak butterflies (whose spiny caterpillars were ubiquitous along sidewalks and roadways during the summers). Inspired, by fifth grade I had determined that a career in zoology would be my profession. This commitment never waned, so when it came time to pursue college, my decision was based solely on a national ranking my brother gave me on universities that excelled in the biological sciences. The University of California was at the top of that list and I applied there with little or no back up plan. I was admitted, and then began a journey that takes me to the core thesis of this essay about learning.

A Diversity of People and Ideas

The Bay Area of California was unlike anything I could have imagined when I arrived there for my first classes. The people, the trees and plants, the smell of the air and the omnipresence of ocean were disorienting but enthralling as well. I dove into my classes and survived one of the great competitive challenges of my life, one I was only prepared for out of a sense of perseverance. I have always felt that I learned my first great lesson for the work I do as an administrator while there: a sense of tolerance for ideas that differ from my own. I met the mainstream and the fringe in this environment, and I came to know almost every facet of human diversity during that time. I became increasingly comfortable with the unpredictable nature of the new ideas that surrounded me and the diversity of people who generated them. In fact, I grew to depend upon these ideas to spur innovation in my own thinking.

My intrigue with Nature remained central to my career motivations and, while still an undergraduate, I received an award to travel abroad and study Africanized ("killer") honeybees in Central America. This experience ultimately sealed my fate as an ecologist in graduate school. Once again, only now in the Dry Forest of northern Costa Rica, I found myself in an environment where I had never been before and with people who spoke a language not native to my tongue. I only prospered from this experience, though, and it further convinced me of the importance of knowing human diversity. This was also my first international experience and laid the groundwork for my own interest in involving students in undergraduate research while in an international setting. (I have helped to lead a National Science Foundation funded "Research Experiences for Undergraduates" program for over a decade that is based in the Republic of Turkey and Greece and where my colleagues and I take students to investigate questions relating to biological invasions.)

These experiences, among people from different locales, have taught me a central lesson about learning, which is that it often requires a different framework of mind to begin the learning process, one that is freer of preconceptions.

I continued graduate school on the same campus where I was an undergraduate and became more intensely focused on my interests in field research. My thesis work required me to travel throughout Northern California and, later, as a post-doctoral associate, I worked on Santa Cruz Island, among the Channel Islands, off the coast of Southern California. Combined with my scientific work today, in two countries where I am not yet fluent in the respective languages (Greek and Turkish), my sense of diversity in people has grown further, affirming a core belief about the value of understanding different people through an appreciation for their customs and ideas. It is gratifying, decades later, to see the same effects in the students I take abroad as part of my own studies.

These experiences, among people from different locales, have taught me a central lesson about learning, which is that it often requires a different framework of mind to begin the learning process, one that is freer of preconceptions. The idea of examining one's own assumptions is a key part of this lesson. Francis Bacon tackled this issue with his notion of the Four Idols.[1] These included the Cave, Tribe, Marketplace, and Theatre. The Idols of the Cave relate to one's own personal biases, the Tribe to group biases, the Marketplace to the currency of conversation (diction), and the Theatre to the impact of larger social assumptions. Bacon's insight was that we are seldom, if ever, in the same state of comprehension with those around us due to our assumptions— something I believe thoughtful faculty members keep in mind as they teach a group of students.

A Career in Teaching and Learning

A major component of the thesis of my essay emerges from my life experience as an academic. In my own field, the idea of a (scientific) process through which one acquires knowledge took a long time to feel completely comfortable with. Most introductions to college include large survey courses where information is relayed to the students without much emphasis on the learning process itself. As a freshman, I took an introductory chemistry class that was so large (over 500 seats in the lecture hall) that it was impractical to even ask a question of the professor, much less expect an in-depth discussion. This approach to learning, referred to as the *vademecum* by Ludwik Fleck,[2] is often not experience-based and does not accommodate the student who wants to challenge the professor. (This, incidentally, did not stop a group of us from daring one another to shout questions to the professor as he stood on the revolving stage far below us.)

My haven in undergraduate school was a work-study job in a laboratory that introduced me to another approach to understanding knowledge and that later spurred my enthusiasm for introducing students to research at an early point in their own careers. Now routinely referred to as "undergraduate research," a high-impact educational practice as defined by Kuh,[3] it creates an interaction between the student and faculty member that encourages another, more open-ended dimension to learning. At the time, and through much of my career, this collision between the "right" or "wrong" mentality of traditional classroom teaching practices with the open-ended inquiry of research was hard to resolve for me. As time has taught me, though, an emphasis on assuming a single correct answer to a question rarely characterizes the mindset of the best contributors to scientific progress (and in other disciplines).

Nobel Laureates, for example, are famous for breaking down existing notions of knowledge (the antithesis of Fleck's *vademecum*), as well illustrated in Medawar's classic advice to young scientists.[4] A poignant and recent example of this was the case of Sir John Gurdon who received the Nobel Prize in Medicine or Physiology in 2012. As he acknowledged receiving the award at a press conference, he noted that his grade report from Eton College stated that his interest in science was "quite ridiculous" based on his poor performance in the traditional classroom setting.

A Eureka Moment

We all have eureka moments. And one of mine occurred over a decade and a half ago when I invited a colleague to our campus to discuss a conclusion that many people were at least somewhat familiar with but that he had drawn an opposing conclusion about years before. Specifically, he had opposed the popular notion that honeybees use a language to communicate to other bees the distance and direction of food (nectar or pollen) from their hive. After his presentation, he was asked about his ability to persist with such an idea in the face of widespread criticism and he responded by noting that he had "a comfort with uncertainty." I have never forgotten those words and have borrowed them as the title for this essay. This idea is, in my opinion, the essence of learning: to distinguish the process of discovery from extant (and assumed) knowledge.[5] This requires crossing a cognitive bridge from a process of just gathering together existing knowledge to one that generates new knowledge. Along the way, one must eventually realize that the absence of an answer to a question, or solution to a problem, is a reasonable state of knowledge and should be expected in the process of inquiry.

> *He responded by noting that he had "a comfort with uncertainty"...This idea is, in my opinion, the essence of learning: to distinguish the process of discovery from extant (and assumed) knowledge.*

The idea that there may not be an immediate answer to every question is one of the most difficult things to teach students. Although we emphasize critical thinking to students, we also emphasize the need to have discrete answers on examinations that we can evaluate and use to assign grades. It turns out that this approach to learning produces different challenges for the learner and may even explain the commonly observed phenomenon that students with average classroom performances can still have excellent aptitudes for research. (Examples include Gregor Mendel and Louis Pasteur.) Open-ended inquiries that we often emphasize outside the classroom are inappropriately termed soft skills when, in fact, these skills are responsible for producing the new knowledge that students are eventually required to learn from textbook-based introductory lectures. Perhaps, instead of suggesting through our teaching methods that learning produces distinct outcomes suitable for examinations, we should emphasize the value of inquiry. Such approaches abound in the literature.[6]

This dichotomy in approaches to learning is why, I suspect, I have been an advocate for learning that occurs beyond the textbook. Not that this approach should be a substitute for the former approach but used sufficiently often that students can understand the value of inquiry, free of assumptions, to create in them a comfort with uncertainty and enjoyment from the realizations that can accompany inquiry-based learning. This, in retrospect, was the dichotomy that confronted me as a student: traditional classroom learning versus the research I conducted working with faculty members. Having encountered this circumstance as a student back then, I feel comfortable with it as an important ingredient in undergraduate education today.

An Institutional Model

At the University of Central Oklahoma (UCO), we have been on more than a decade-long journey to better understand and implement transformative learning practices;[7] results from these kinds of practices consistently demonstrate that students who engage in them will complete their degrees more often than others who do not do so and gain other career benefits as well (see an overview for STEM disciplines[8]). Recent findings of the Student Transformative Learning Record (STLR) demonstrate that positive and widespread responses by students to these practices have occurred during the last three years on the UCO campus.[9] A better integration of these practices with the classroom environment is invited through the tenant referred to as Disciplinary Knowledge. By creating this inquiry-based interface with knowledge more often and earlier in a student's career, we can hope to break down these seemingly contradictory approaches to the educational experience of our undergraduate students.

We have made consistent efforts to encourage inquiry through a new Office of High Impact Practices (OHIP) at UCO.[10] OHIP encouraged 89 students this year (2019) to attend the annual National Conference on Undergraduate Research (NCUR) near Atlanta, Georgia. (Just last year, this conference was held on the UCO campus and attracted the third highest number of participants in the thirty-plus year history of the event.) This is a dramatic increase from previous years and will help to further embed an expectation of promoting inquiry-base processes for our students. My participation in this institutional transition has not been accidental and is consistent with my desire to see students feel more comfortable with inquiry. An entire national organization, the Council on Undergraduate Research (CUR), advances this same idea and has seen considerable growth in participant numbers in recent years, as well as greater acceptance across disciplines.

My own view of learning has taken two decades of formal education and another two decades of teaching experience to come to the conclusion I have drawn in this essay. The emergence of students from content-rich educational experiences can leave them with less aptitude for learning as a process. It should not be frustrating to see that this transition takes time because both forms of learning are needed in one's lifetime. However, the use of high-impact practices at an earlier age will ensure that a comfort with inquiry develops sooner in students' lives and will be used more effectively, after their formal education, to further their careers.

A comfort with uncertainty can only be created, in my experience, through involvement in two practices. First, exposure to new ideas, often by meeting people with different backgrounds than our own, needs to be encouraged early and often with our students. Secondly, an earlier introduction to inquiry-based practices should be employed to lessen the discomfort that can develop with students when they do not have an immediate answer to a given question. A university campus is an ideal setting to create these circumstances for students. Indeed, most university campuses have a wide array of students from different backgrounds and can create the curriculum and high-impact educational practices needed to accomplish this goal. Learning as a process is not alien to faculty members on any university campus, but the active encouragement of this approach through curriculum and faculty-mentored activities will certainly enhance the opportunity for it to occur, as I believe it has for me.

JOHN F. BARTHELL

John F. Barthell, Ph.D. (University of California at Berkeley) is provost and vice president for academic affairs at the University of Central Oklahoma where he leads the university's highly-regarded faculty with a focus on undergraduate research, fostering an innovative learning community, and transforming students through transformative learning practices. Barthell served UCO for 18 years before being named provost with seven of those years as dean of the College of Mathematics and Science. He established the Center for Undergraduate Research and Education in STEM (science, technology, engineering, and math), and he has served as the principal investigator of multiple National Science Foundation grants. In 2003, Barthell received the Neely Excellence in Teaching award.

CHAPTER SIX

Tess Remy-Schumacher, Ph.D.

Challenge or Contentment

The Biggest and Loudest Instrument!

Music has always been a major part of my life. As a kindergarten student, age five, I walked to my neighbors' house every day. They had a "magic" piano. With the help of my friend I learned to play piano. I kept begging my parents to have my own instrument. Finally, they conceded and took me to the local music school to choose an instrument I could learn.

I was immediately drawn to the cello and selected it because it was the biggest and loudest instrument I could find. The cello seemed to speak to me with a dark and haunting voice which immediately connected with my soul, changing my life forever.

A Dream Comes True

I was very fortunate to study with great teachers who enabled me to start playing concerts at a very early age. At the age of seven, I performed my first solo concerto with orchestra. I understood early on that there is "no pain, no gain;" the demands of preparing for concerts and the nervousness before the performances seemed to be the price for the exciting opportunity to be on stage and perform for an audience. Yearly competitions added another very challenging component to my early life and career. I always rejected the idea of "competing against fellow musicians." However, a musical career, scholarships and concerts are almost impossible without participating in the draining competition life.

During these early years, my hero and model had always been the famous British cellist, Jacqueline Du Pre. Her cello seemed to sing with an unlimited amount of expressions and feelings. She also was one of the first female cellists to make a career in a very male-dominated domain. This naturally added to my great admiration. In 1965, Jaqueline had become famous with her interpretation and recording of Edgar Elgar's Cello Concerto with Sir John Barbirolli and the London Symphony Orchestra. Shortly after, she married conductor and pianist Daniel Barenboim. Their recordings of all major works of the cello repertoire are still considered the greatest interpretation and performance of these works to this day. By the time I was a teenager,

Jacqueline Du Pre had already stopped performing due to the progression of multiple sclerosis. My dream, however, was still to study with her! After I kept begging her agency to let me audition for her, she accepted me as her last student in London after hearing me play.

Facing the Challenge…and Heartache

Preparing for my move to London in 1984 occupied all my thoughts. Feelings of excitement to meet and study with my idol oscillated between feelings of fear of moving to a foreign country without financial resources or a place to live. I had accepted a part time position in a professional orchestra already as a teenager. I knew that for the first months I had to commute each week for my lessons between Cologne and London while keeping my job in Cologne.

Finally, the day for my first trip to London had arrived. I took a night train to Oostende, Belgium, changed to a night ferry to Dover, sleeping in the ship's basement next to my cello, and then continued by train to London to head to my first lesson.

I still remember my excitement standing in front of "Chepstow Villas" in London about to meet Jacqueline for the first time. Being a typical German, I was early, and when my 11:00 a.m. appointment time was close, I collected all my courage to ring the doorbell. The moment had come to meet Jacqueline in person. I had prepared the Elgar Cello Concerto for her.

> *The time studying with her was one of the most transformational experiences in my life. I learned that each person has a choice on which attitude and road to take, no matter how brutally fate may intervene.*

Suddenly, I became very self-conscious playing the same concerto which had started her career and fame while she was confined to a wheelchair. She could not even hold her cello anymore. Jacqueline must have read my mind; with the biggest smile and kindness she said: *"I'm so looking forward to hear you play my concerto. I haven't heard my cello for so long. Could you get my Strad (ivarius) out of the corner and play your lesson on my cello?"* (Coincidentally, this Stradivarius Cello was later purchased by my American Cello Professor and distinguished concert cellist Lynn Harrell).

The time studying with her was one of the most transformational experiences in my life. I learned that each person has a choice on which attitude and road to take, no matter how brutally fate may intervene. It was heart breaking to see my idol suffering and unable to perform. But Jacqueline always chose challenge over giving up or even contentment. At every moment, even with her increasing disability during my year of study, she revealed and shared a monumental passion for music and teaching. Her love for music and people fulfilled her life until the very end. She passed away on October 19, 1987, at the age of forty-two.

During my London year, I learned that no matter what life "throws at you," standing up to challenges instead of giving in to a status quo is the only way to grow and lead a fulfilling life. While I felt the magnitude of the experience studying with Jacqueline du Pre at the time, I only realized much later how much my "London year" had transformed me. I felt a new and deep gratitude for being able to play the cello, make music and perform for and communicate with an audience. This gratitude provided me with energy and tenacity for the tens of thousands of hours of practice to come, dealing with the stress of concert tours, and later facing the challenge of keeping up a performance recording career while fulfilling a demanding life as a university professor and academic.

Passing It On

I feel tremendously fortunate for the opportunity to study with Jacqueline Du Pre. To this day, I treasure all her technical advice for fingerings, bowings and musical suggestions. They are permanently written into my performance scores. I am happy to share these experiences with many of my students.

While my students are talented and kind, I have noticed a need amongst most students for more tenacity and persistence in developing their artistry and personal growth. Sometimes the "easy way out" seems to create a sense of contentment. I sense a hesitation and fear of "giving it all" and of sacrificing for a higher goal.

"Failures" under these conditions are, in reality, experiences towards personal and professional growth. The expectation that learning is supposed to be "easy" bears a multitude of frustrating experiences.

The lingering question seems to be: "what happens if I fail?" Only facing challenges and undergoing sacrifices will offer a chance for fulfillment. "Failures" under these conditions are, in reality, experiences towards personal and professional growth. The expectation that learning is supposed to be "easy" bears a multitude of frustrating experiences.

I remember one particular visit I made to a public school to work with the cello section in the orchestra. I gave some suggestions for improvement to the cellists. When they did not see an immediate effect, I sensed much frustration. When I questioned my young colleagues about this rather immature reaction, the response was *"I thought I was not talented, because I could not do it right away."*

At the time I shared the example how infants learn to walk and their relentless and countless attempts to do so until "their brains have figured it out." I shared my own experiences during my studies with Russian cellist Boris Pergamenschikow. During one lesson I stated that my Haydn Concerto was far from perfection after one month of practicing five hours daily. His response was simple: "You need to practice it for six months, eight hours a day to have a better chance!"

It has been a priority in my teaching to encourage my students to pursue their dreams and never to let contentment be in the way of achieving personal and artistic excellence. Challenge and life-long learning, not short cuts, are the way to realize dreams.

A Student for Life

Being a student is a challenge. Remaining a student for life is the biggest but necessary challenge for any educator. In 2010, I had the unique opportunity to be a Visiting Fellow and Visiting Scholar at Harvard University. Waiting for my first seminar with Dr. Robert Levin felt like a flashback to standing in front of Jacqueline du Pre's door for the first time. At Harvard, I had the unique opportunity to enter a new world of historical performance practice and to study baroque cello. This experience ultimately led to my establishment of the Brisch Center for Historical Performance together with my colleague, Dr. Ted Honea.

Epilogue

I believe that students need to have a good professional foundation. They need to learn their craft and the material of their individual discipline. But only the emotional and psychological preparedness for challenge and sacrifices lead to a fulfilling life.

I would like to conclude with my most challenging recent experience in this regard: the premiere performance and recording of David Maslanka's Cello Concerto "Remember Me." In 2013, Dr. Brian Lamb, conductor of the UCO Wind Symphony, and I were part of a commissioning consortium for a cello concerto by the Montana composer David Maslanka. The first information I received was the musical score. The beauty of the completed score was overwhelming. Only later did I receive the liner notes and narration describing the horrific scene of the killing of a Jewish family during the Holocaust. Struggling with this contrast created a tremendous challenge for me. I ultimately understood that David Maslanka's mission with this composition was to demonstrate music's healing effects on the human soul: "Musical Vibration heals." My feelings of pain and suffering and horror were healed and transformed to beauty through Maslanka's music.

Shortly after the premiere, I felt the necessity to share this experience with more people and bring the concerto to young students in particular. My public schools concert initiative and CD recording "Music for Peace" were born.

My research assistant, Buyun Li, and I performed twenty school concerts and asked the students to write down their thoughts after our presentation. These documents are among the most emotional testimonies about the healing power of music that I have ever read. I would like to include three of these statements:

"Dear Mr. Maslanka, I don't think I can describe how beautiful and inspiring your piece was. I can't remember the last time I heard something so impactful. Listening to "Remember Me" brought sorrow, joy, and hope to my heart. It is truly a work of art. Sitting here I remember the time in my life when I was at my lowest. On February 24, 2014, I sat in the hospital and watched the green light flatten as my uncle passed away. I don't recall ever going through something so traumatic in my 15 years of living. It hurts me every day to know that I have to go another day without him, but after hearing your story and listening to "Remember Me," I think to finally have hope again, and thanks to you! In a time of such destruction and horror, there is also joy and hope, a lesson I have now learned. Thank you for inspiring me and enlightening me with such beauty. Music is truly the key to our emotions."

***

"I am not experienced enough in life to relate to some things as tragic as this piece was written of. However, I could experience the emotions that were portrayed by the cello and the piano. The duo played with such eloquence and feeling. The lullaby in the middle felt like a surreal moment in life where you aren't in the moment but just watching over. Beautiful piece and it makes me wish I played the cello."

***

"I loved the piece. I wanted to be a songwriter and make my own music pieces, but I didn't get a lot of motivation about the career. And when I listened to the song it gave me a lot of motivation to pick myself up and become my dream. Sometimes I wonder when I'm frustrated how do people do it, and through this piece I heard and felt the hard work, the motivation, and I felt something I haven't felt before. I'm still trying to point out what it is, but I just want to say thank you for lifting me up from quitting my dream. This song has given me hope that someday I could be making beautiful music like you. You have inspired me to stop quitting on the hard things and continue doing what I love even though it's hard."

Currently we are preparing a Germany Concert Tour with Dr. Brian Lamb, the UCO Wind Symphony and myself, performing "Remember Me" in the UNESCO World Heritage site "Stiftsbasilika Waldsassen" and the International Festival "Sandstein Festival" in Dresden. I want to share with my students and others that life is always a journey and that facing challenges is the way to ultimate happiness and fulfilling one's dreams.

Final Thoughts

I sincerely thank my students, colleagues and audiences for keeping me challenged. I thank Dr. Neely and his family for their ongoing support and inspiration to be the best teacher possible. I also thank my friend, creative writer, Angela Morris, for her professional edits to my document. Most of all, I thank my husband David, for his love and support always. Thank you also, David, for countless edits and for challenging my musical and scientific brain to activate my language neurons!

TESS REMY-SCHUMACHER

Dr. Tess Remy-Schumacher, born in Cologne, Germany, received her MM and DMA as "most outstanding graduate of the year for performance, academic excellence and leadership," at the University of Southern California. Among her teachers were the legendary Jacqueline du Pre, Boris Pergamenschikow, Siegfried Palm, Lynn Harrell, Eleonore Schoenfeld and the Amadeus Quartet. She has been a concert soloist for many years, performing and recording in Asia, Australia, Europe and the U.S., including the Wigmore Hall, Jubilee Hall, Carnegie Recital Hall, and Bradley Hall. Among her 12 CD recordings, she most recently recorded Cello Concertos by David Maslanka and Carter Pann with the UCO Wind Symphony and Dr. Brian Lamb. Following her appointment at James Cook University, Australia, she is now a Professor of Cello, Baroque Cello, and Co-Founder and General Program Coordinator of the Brisch Center for Historical Performance Practice at UCO. From 2010-2012 she was a Visiting Fellow Performance and Visiting Scholar at Harvard University. In 2007, Remy-Schumacher received the Neely Excellence in Teaching award.
www.tessremy.com

7 CHAPTER SEVEN

Cheryl B. Frech, Ph.D.

A Long and Winding Road: A Teaching Journey

I did not set out to be a teacher or to have a quarter-century (and counting) career in higher education. Like most young people, I was not thinking very much about my future when I was in high school. I did well in school, and often found myself as one of the few girls in science and math classes. I also was deeply involved with music and I struggled to choose between a career in music and a career in the sciences.

A bit of background: both my parents went to college. My father has a Ph.D. in chemistry and my mother has a bachelor's degree in elementary education. They were first-generation college students shortly after World War II, and both of my father's siblings also graduated from college. My mother taught first grade until I was born, and my father worked in the chemical industry. We lived in southern California and my mother used her elementary education background to provide a rich educational environment in the home—there were a lot of books, educational activities, trips to museums, and workshops. Our family moved to Oklahoma City in 1970, shortly after my younger sister was born.

When it was time to go to college, I didn't look very far, and enrolled at Oklahoma State University in 1977. You had to select a major when you enrolled, so I looked through the handouts and selected biochemistry, since I liked both biology and chemistry. I kept up my involvement with music for two years, playing in the marching band for a year and two years in the concert band. I finally relinquished band when the laboratory courses in my major began taking up too much time to do both. I cruised along in college, still not thinking intentionally about what I would do after graduation. After my sophomore year, I had a summer job doing analytical chemistry at an oil company research center and enjoyed the work.

When I came home for the winter break of my senior year, everyone was asking, "What will you do when you graduate in May?" I had no idea and panic set in. My final undergraduate semester might have been the most stressful time in my life. I interviewed for industrial jobs and took the GRE (graduate school in chemistry?) and the GMAT (perhaps an MBA?). At seemingly the eleventh hour, I decided to pursue a graduate degree in chemistry at the University of Oklahoma.

As a graduate student, you are supported as a teaching assistant for the first several years until your major advisor picks you up on a grant to be a research assistant. So, I found myself as a 21-year-old graduate student standing in front of laboratory sections of General Chemistry I students, most of whom were barely younger than me, and I loved it. Graduate students also have to present various seminars to the department and their graduate committee. The first time I presented a seminar, one of my committee members said, "You explained this topic very well. Have you considered teaching?" I brushed the comment off until the next seminar, when a similar comment was made. As my fellow graduate students were finishing up their degrees, most of them were being hired in the chemical industry. Since my father had also worked in industry, I assumed I would be looking for industrial jobs soon.

As the saying goes, "Life is what happens when you make other plans." I had met my future husband at OU—Roger was a professor of chemistry and we were married shortly before I finished my Ph.D. Taking a job with a chemical company far from Oklahoma just didn't seem to be possible. Upon graduation, I completed two research post-docs, one at OU and one in Germany, where we spent an exciting year doing research at the Max Planck Polymer Institute in Mainz. I still did not know what my career was going to be. When we returned to Oklahoma, I took a position as a Visiting Assistant Professor of Chemistry at OU. My assignment was two large lecture sections of General Chemistry each semester. Despite the challenges of teaching more than 200 students in an auditorium setting (before the advent of the technology we have today), I realized I would make my career in teaching. When the position of "General Chemistry Coordinator" was advertised at UCO, I applied and was hired.

If teaching is a journey, everything I did before I came to UCO was preparation for my journey: packing the suitcase, studying the route, strengthening my body, taking scouting trips. The first two years at UCO were idyllic. I was so happy teaching and organizing the General Chemistry courses that I honestly would forget that I also got a paycheck.

A teaching journey, however, does not stand apart from the rest of your life. Who you are as a teacher is impacted by what happens in your life. Your life journey and your teaching journey are usually on parallel tracks, except when something in one area overlaps into the other area or changes you in some fundamental way.

The second year I taught at OU, I was pregnant, but became very ill and had a stillborn baby at 5 months. Aside from the grief that my husband and I shared, this event changed me as a person and a teacher. Like many young women, I had assumed that once you get to a certain point in a pregnancy, a baby will be born and off you go. The concept of being close to death and losing a child had never entered my mind. I did recover, but it took some time to regain my physical and mental health.

The second year I taught at UCO, I was pregnant again. Of course, this time I was terrified. Again, I experienced some major complications, but as the due date drew near, Roger said, "At some point you have to start believing in this baby." Our daughter was born in February 1993 and I returned to teaching in the fall semester that year. Our second daughter was born without any complications whatsoever (but three weeks early) in 1995. I took unpaid leave of absence for a semester so we could bond as a family, and I returned to UCO in the Spring 1996 semester.

Having serious health issues changed how I interact with students who find themselves in situations where their health or the health of a loved one is in question. Students (and faculty colleagues) sometimes insist they will be just fine to return to work or school very soon after an accident or illness. My response is always, "Take all the time you need." Work and school will be here for you to return to. It's much more important to get back your physical, mental, and spiritual health.

By the late 1990s, I had moved from being a young faculty member with no children, to a mom-aged faculty member with two small children, commuting at least 45 minutes each way from Norman to Edmond every day. Since both Roger and I were faculty members who had to meet our classes and attend to university responsibilities, we hired an older woman as a nanny to care for our children in our home four days a week. Our children would be in their home environment if they got sick and they had each other. One day a week I drove the kids to Oklahoma City to spend the day with their grandparents while I went to work at UCO.

With my little family launched, I could return to the exploration of teaching and learning. Those colleagues of mine in graduate school who had taken jobs in the chemical industry asked, "How do you teach the same thing every semester?" I was flabbergasted. Even though, by now, I have taught General Chemistry I and II lectures and laboratories more than 50 times each, the course is *never* the same. The students change, you change, the world changes. Each course is filled with unique interactions. And as Parker Palmer points out in *The Courage to Teach*, middle age comes quickly for faculty. Each year the students in your freshman classroom are generally around 18 years old and you are

(n + 1) years old, where n is the age you were when you first started teaching. The cultural and societal connections between you and the students in your classroom become more of a generation gap each year. Every year you adjust.

Two things happened in the late 1990s that impacted who I am as a faculty member and an instructor. First, I had been active in the Oklahoma Section of the American Chemical Society (ACS) since I arrived at UCO, serving in several offices. Being active in the professional chemistry community is one of my priorities. In 1997 I attended a national ACS meeting with a senior UCO colleague, Terry Smith. Terry was the councilor of our Oklahoma Section and had been active in the ACS for many years. Accompanying him at an ACS national meeting that had more than 10,000 attendees was like watching a master at work. He knew so many people and he had mastered the ins and outs of symposia, poster sessions, governance, and town halls. He also introduced me to what seemed like hundreds of people. Terry encouraged me to volunteer to serve on a national ACS examination committee that works on a version of a national standardized exam for chemistry.

The cultural and societal connections between you and the students in your classroom become more of a generational gap each year. Every year you adjust.

Secondly, in 1998 I attended my first Biennial Conference on Chemical Education to continue my examination committee work. What a treat to be at a conference where everyone was talking about how to teach chemistry! Here I met a new colleague who also took me under her wing and introduced me to many people. By serving on a national exam committee for the ACS, I was able to interact with chemistry educators at all levels, as well as textbook authors, and members of the chemical education community. I learned how a national examination is created— from the topic matrix, to question construction, to the trial exam statistics.

The exam committees met and worked together at national ACS meetings and the Biennial Conferences on Chemical Education. I started attending sessions on chemical education: how do students learn chemistry? What are some of the best practices? And suddenly, I had ideas to try in my classroom in Oklahoma. The most significant thing I learned about and began to try was Team-Based Learning (TBL). Course material is divided into modules and each module follows a cycle of preparation, in-class readiness assessment, a team exercise, and an overall assessment of the material. Students are responsible for both their own learning and the progress of their team.

Trying a technique in your classroom is not quite as easy as it sounds. Every new thing you try essentially has to go through the scientific method. Hypothesis, test, analyze, revise. What happens when something goes wrong? This was before UCO had established a strong center for teaching and learning, so I checked in with Dee Fink, a renowned educational expert, and also a friend and colleague in Norman, and asked for his help. After many iterations, I finally found a team-based learning system that worked for UCO students, our class sizes and setup, and me.

Going to BCCEs and ACS national meetings connected me to the larger world of chemistry educators. Opportunities emerged. I was asked to sit on national committees for ACS and the ACS Division of Chemical Education. I had opportunities to work with publishers on educational materials. I told the editor of the *Journal of Chemical Education* that I would like to be their book and media review editor someday, and in 2008, I began to serve in that capacity. After almost two decades of activity, in 2016 I was elected Chair of the ACS Division of Chemical Education.

I have been going to meetings, learning things about chemistry education, trying them in the classroom, making adjustments, presenting posters and workshops on what I have learned, and become a seasoned faculty member. I have done as much at UCO, with the local ACS section, and at the regional and national level with ACS, the Division of Chemical Education, and the *Journal of Chemical Education* as I can.

> *How else to best help students on their journey? I have come to understand that teaching students how to learn is the most important thing I can teach them.*

But perhaps I had not done enough to help UCO students directly. Other faculty members were doing hands-on laboratory research with students at UCO, but I was not. What could I give back to the students that would benefit them similarly? In 2014, our department created two Professionalism in Chemistry courses for our majors. I began teaching Professionalism in Chemistry I in 2015. Students in this course learn about what it means to be an emerging professional in chemistry (or in any field). They prepare a resume, practice networking skills, discuss science in the news, explore ethics and safety at a level beyond their regular classes, and attend professional science meetings in the area. With the development of this course, I feel I finally have been able to model, mentor, and guide students into the intangibles of the field. This is what I have strived to be: a chemical professional in education.

How else to best help students on their journey? I have come to understand that teaching students *how to learn* is the most important thing I can teach them. Teaching chemistry is not enough. In the past few years, I have been teaching them about metacognition and Bloom's taxonomy. Each quiz that they take is followed up with a learning reflection. Early results seem promising, and students are coming back to tell me how useful these skills are.

Somehow, I moved from new faculty member, to mid-career faculty member, to senior faculty member. I went from wannabe mother, to mother of small children, to seeing both of our daughters attend college and graduate. I went from seeking approval from my department chair, to being the department chair, to mentoring a new department chair. I went from being introduced to people at ACS meetings, to introducing and mentoring others. Transformation occurs for all of us on a teaching journey. Some years ago, I learned the phrase, "Send the elevator back down." We have all benefited from the wisdom and opportunities provided by others. Be sure to help facilitate your colleagues' and students' transformative journeys by sending the elevator back down when you can.

Over the years, I have seen colleagues come and go. The academic life is definitely not for everyone. The "boom and bust" cycle of the semesters can be both wearing and wearying. It's hard to go to a movie or a special event on a Tuesday evening, and you really only get to take a vacation in the summer. Some young faculty have come in and decided to pursue another career. I have seen colleagues retire, some early, some very late. I hope that I will be able to step away soon, while I have time to travel and enjoy time with my husband.

Here are a few closing thoughts about how to become and remain engaged on your own teaching journey:

- Cultivate your teaching buddies—people with whom you can talk about teaching, bounce ideas around with, and share strategies.
- Recognize that life inside the classroom reflects life outside of the classroom, for you and for students. Be kind, share what you can, and listen.
- Keep up with what is important to you. Music is still a part of my life: I play two instruments regularly, take lessons, perform occasionally, and joined a handbell choir when I was in my 50s.
- Celebrate the journey. If you stay in academia, you grow as an educator,

as a faculty member, and as a professional. Mark the mileposts—
commencements, convocations, new building dedications, retirements,
and new hires—just as you simultaneously mark your life's journeys—
weddings, funerals, births, and holidays. Your travel journal is a tapestry
of both.

CHERYL B. FRECH

Cheryl Baldwin Frech is a professor of chemistry at the University of
Central Oklahoma, where she has taught since 1991. She served as
department chair from 2004–2012. Cheryl is active in the American
Chemical Society at the local, regional, and national level and was named
an ACS Fellow in 2014. She was the first recipient of the Neely Award in
1999.

8 CHAPTER EIGHT

Mohamed Bingabr, Ph.D.

A Journey of an International Student in an American University

Anthropologists determined that the first human migration was from Africa to the south of Arabia, which is currently known as Yemen. Some settled there while others continued the journey north. I am the descendent of the people who stayed in Yemen—either because they lacked the spirit of exploration or had most likely taken over the land, thus pushing their brethren to continue immigrating. Not unlike the original immigrants, I have my own migration story, however, my destination was the United States to pursue a degree in engineering in 1985. Now, I am a professor and the Chair of the Engineering and Physics department at the University of Central Oklahoma (UCO). In this essay, I will share my personal educational journey in America, which led me to become the person I am today. I will focus on the impact of good teachers on students, the challenges faced by international students such as language and culture differences, and finally the impact of education on society. Through this essay, I hope new international students will have an inkling of the challenges awaiting them, American educators will understand the challenges faced by international students, and politicians will understand the impact of education in bridging gaps between different cultures and ideologies.

My first encounter with America was in 1975 when I came to Dearborn, Michigan, for an ear surgery. I had a ruptured eardrum and chronic ear infections from infancy and had grown up using stinging alcohol eardrops for cleaning. Because of my ear problems, I used to open my mouth in order to hear well. People thought I was mentally challenged, and they used to feel sorry for my parents. My performance in elementary school was poor and my mother used to cry and yell at me when I continued to be ranked among the last in the class. In second grade, I was ranked 35th in the class which made my mother upset. I remember her asking me why I could not be ranked high in the class like my cousins instead of being the last. I promptly stopped crying and informed her that there were two other students ranked below me. She stopped yelling and started laughing at my innocent response, then finished bathing me, and I felt victorious. Mothers always see their children as the smartest and most beautiful ones, and my mother could not understand why her child's performance was poor. She never went to school, and she did not know that my hearing problem was preventing me from understanding the teachers in crowded noisy classes.

Thankfully, I was finally diagnosed and the doctors in Yemen told my father that tympanic and middle ear reconstructions were being performed successfully in the U.S. I was ten years old when I arrived at the Detroit airport on June 1975 and was immediately struck with the many differences in this new country. I was blown away by everything, from how green it was to how clean the streets were and how fully stocked the supermarkets were with candy and drinks. My uncle had a small restaurant in Dearborn, which served Yemeni laborers from the Ford car factory. A month after arriving, I received successful surgeries in both ears and started hearing better and even made many friends. After three months, the time came to go back to Yemen leaving me with mixed feelings. On one hand, I didn't want to leave my new friends, the full candy store, and the arcade games; but on the other hand, I missed my mother and family back in Yemen. When I arrived at JFK airport, I cried knowing that this was the end of my new world.

After I returned to Yemen, my mom used to notice my sadness at leaving America and would try to comfort me by saying, "you can finish high school with high grades and get a scholarship to go back to America." Her words were the motivation I needed to achieve my dreams through education. With time, I reacclimated to my old life and quickly went back to playing soccer on the dirt field, but this time I could hear my friends clearly and my performance in school improved. In seventh grade, I had a math teacher who enjoyed teaching and came to class excited as if he had a revelation to teach us. He was always engaging students in discussion and gave us the impression that we were challenging him with our intelligent questions. He used to take pride in what he wore and the impressions he made on us every day. He made me love math and enjoy solving problems as if I am solving puzzles. He believed in me, and more importantly, he made me believe that I could have a great future, which led me to be an engineer and educator. On the other end of the spectrum, I had a chemistry teacher who showed up to class as if he was forced to come and always complained about us and cursed his luck for being a teacher. When we asked him questions about certain chemical reactions, he would respond with "that's the way things are," and we should memorize it as it is. I always found chemistry a mystery to me with no discernable logic, which is one of the reasons I pursued engineering instead of medicine. Students can sense the energy and enthusiasm of the teacher the moment he/she enters the classroom and that will determine whether students become engaged or spend their time counting down the minutes until the lecture is over. In 1984, upon high school graduation, I received the highest score in math—198 of 200 out of the whole nation. The U.S. used to give 10 scholarships to developing countries like Yemen. I was awarded one of these scholarships to study engineering at Syracuse University in New York. I was excited about my opportunity, but also anxious about leaving family, living alone, and overcoming the language barrier.

I arrived at Syracuse University in 1985 with two students, Abdu and Ali from Yemen, who enrolled in the computer engineering program. We were teenagers and we had mixed feelings about America. We were excited to see the America we learned about from Hollywood movies, like James Bond, but at the same time, we were worried from the America we learned about from political news. In the seventies and eighties, the Israel-Palestine struggle was at its peak. In Yemen, we saw one side of the struggle: Israel destroying Palestinians' homes, jailing them, and killing them. The U.S. is the main supporter to Israel, providing them with weapons and money while vetoing any help to the Palestinians in the United Nation. We were worried that the teachers would be racist against us because we were Muslims and Arabs. We met students from Yemen who came before us and other students from the Gulf States, Egypt, Palestine, Lebanon, Morocco, and Algeria. We used to meet in the cafeteria and talk about teachers' teaching styles and their backgrounds. The older students told us to switch out of the Calculus 1 section we were in because the teacher was Jewish and hated Arabs. Next day, we went to the register office to change it. Ali was able to switch out, but Abdu and I were not so lucky. Our Arab friends had told us not to criticize or express our distrust of Jewish people in public because they were powerful and controlled America. For that reason, we did not tell the advisor the true reason for wanting to change the section, so she refused to change our section because there was no time conflict with other courses in our schedule. Abdu and I walked out of her office so despondent and bitter that we concluded that she was either Jewish or a crusader that hated Muslims. Dictators in the Middle East and politicians use religion in politics to create an external enemy to deviate the public's attention from their corruption and failure to improve the economic status of citizens. We came to American universities to learn and become engineers, but we were suspicious of our American teachers. On the contrary and to my surprise, I noticed that Arab and Muslim students who grew up in the United States did not share these feelings, which contributed to the distance between us and them. Students coming from the Middle East used to joke that Arab-Americans are either brainwashed or agents of the CIA.

Our first semester did not go well. On our first day of calculus, we met our Jewish teacher. He was a tall white man with a thick beard (like a typical mathematician), but to us it was the beard of a rabbi, and one who did not like Muslims. He would not talk to us, and we would not ask him for help in homework. Abdu and I used to sit at the back confused, trying to make sense of what he was saying; we couldn't even distinguish when he was explaining calculus and cracking jokes. I would only know he was joking when I heard the students laughing. I still didn't get it but at least I felt relaxed that I missed a joke and not a theory. Students liked him, but we could not understand him because he described the math in plain English, which was good, but as international students, we wanted him to solve problems and use symbols with the least amount of English words possible. This language barrier extended to other classes as well. For example, one time during the physics drill session, Abdu, Ali, and I were sitting next to each other and the teacher asked each one of us to draw the x- and y-axis on the blackboard. We did not know what x- and y-axis meant. The teacher asked the next student who was American, and he went to the blackboard and drew two perpendicular lines and labeled the horizontal line x and the vertical line y. We looked at each other and were shocked about the simple question that we did not understand. We had already learned about the x- and y-axis in the 7th grade. In the second lecture in Physics 1, the professor finished chapter 1. I went home to look at the chapter 1 and found out it was 35 pages long. I started reading the chapter and it took me 4 hours to finish the first page. I translated so many words to Arabic, but the sentences still did not make sense. How was I going to finish 35 pages in two days? I started thinking about failing and how disappointed my parents and family would be. We realized that language would be our biggest challenge. Yes, we met the language requirement and got over 500 in the TOEFL, but the scientific language and spoken dialogue were something different. We were overwhelmed by the challenge and cultural differences, so we gave up and stopped studying altogether.

In addition to language difficulties, we could not adapt to the new culture and lifestyle. We had more freedom from our parents' supervision and more financial independence because of the scholarship; we could come home at any time and do whatever we desired. Our Arab friends who came before us introduced us to all kinds of entertainment and socialization. I lost track of the goal of coming to the U.S., and as a result, I finished the semester with only three courses (two Ds and one C) which was below the required 12 credits to be a full-time student. My second semester ended just as badly as my first one, and that was the case for my two friends, Ali and Abdu. I got a letter from AMEDIST, the agency that manages the scholarships, warning me of terminating my scholarship if I did not improve my GPA. I was devastated, angry with myself, and ashamed of my academic performance. I wished for death so that I wouldn't bring shame to my family. My mother used to brag to her friends that her son was studying in America, and when they asked her what he was studying, she wouldn't know what bioengineering was; to her it was enough that I would be graduating from an American University. I betrayed my father's dream that one day I would be great and serve Yemen. Instead of studying, I followed my desires and wasted a lot of time in socializing. I wished many times that I could have died before my parents found out about my failure.

In the eighties, there were suicide bombs in Israeli cafeterias and buses. In the Arab world, those were considered martyrs fighting occupation and bringing honor to their families. I wished to die like them for a greater cause in order to escape the misery of failing in college and disappointing my parents. At that time, I had a conversation about suicide bombers with one of my friend's mother, Ms. Bermann, who was a very intelligent woman. She managed a house that cared for mentally challenged children. She could not understand how someone could end his life in this way and kill innocent people for a political agenda. I told her if Israel killed any of my family or occupied my country, I would do the same thing. I was lucky that she was a compassionate person and did not report me to the police or the FBI. Instead, she told me, "Mohamed you are too smart to die like that, and you could serve what you believe in better if you work harder to be famous in your field so people will listen to you." It was a long conversation and her words made me think again about my future and gave me the confidence and the belief that I could do better in school. I could be just like the American Jewish people who used their fame and words to help Israel peacefully. I also realized that I had passed all courses with zero effort, so I could do much better if I dedicated my time and energy to school.

> *In my second year of college, my English got better, and I set my goal to learn and succeed no matter what the obstacles were, and most importantly, I learned how to manage my time.*

In my second year of college, my English got better and I set my goal to learn and succeed no matter what the obstacles were, and most importantly, I learned how to manage my time. The first thing I did was cut unnecessary relationships with friends and stop wasting the weekends in socializing. Then, I went to my academic advisor, Dr. Chamberlin, and asked permission to take seven courses (21 credits). He advised me to take only 12 credits and do well to improve my GPA. I insisted on taking 21 credits to compensate for the low credits I took last year. I took 21 credits of engineering and math courses. I finished the semester with all A's and one B, with a GPA of 3.8 for the semester. Dr. Chamberlin met me at the end of the semester with a smile wanting to know how I did it. Time management—I had to develop the self-discipline to tackle homework after classes and only have fun after I finished. I took calculus 3 and 4 with the Jewish teacher and I got an A in both of them. I did so well in his classes that he used to solve some problems in the class and mention that he's doing it the Bingabr way. My experience with him encouraged other Arab students to take calculus with him. I took Bioinstrumentation Lab I and II with Dr. Smith. We used to discuss the Palestinian and Israeli conflict, and even though we had two different views on the best way to solve the problem, we never let it affect our teacher-student relationship. I never felt I was discriminated against because of my religion or outspoken opinion. I found professionalism in my teachers. I found a department and college where you find faculty of different religions and ethnicities—Buddhist, Christian, Jewish, Muslims, Hindus, and Secular. All have respect for each other and share a goal of providing the best education, conducting research, and advancing the mission of the college. That is America.

I finished my baccalaureate in 1989 with a 3.5 GPA and ranked fourth in a class of 16 graduates. If it were not for my performance during the first year, I would have graduated with a higher GPA and maybe ranked second in the class. My automated water pump senior design project was ranked 1st. Dr. Smith was so impressed that he offered me a full teaching assistant scholarship to start my master's, but I decided to go back to Yemen and start my own business. However, after returning, I discovered that Yemen had advanced in the four years I was gone and was already using imported Chinese water pumps, so I ended up working in Sana'a University Hospital. I was the first biomedical engineer in Yemen, and as such, I was energetic to serve my country and worked on installing and maintaining all new medical and laboratory instruments that were received from Kuwait as gift to Sana'a University. Ali and Abdu also went back to Yemen and worked with Texas HUNT Oil and Gas Company in Yemen. After the first gulf war in 1991, the economy in Yemen declined because president Salah of Yemen took side with Saddam Hussein, so I contacted Dr. Chamberlin and Dr. Smith to see if they still needed a teaching assistant for the bioinstrumentation labs. I was in luck because I was awarded a full teaching assistant scholarship at Syracuse University and finished my master's in electrical engineering with 3.8 GPA. After completing my master's degree, I went back to Yemen in 1993 and worked as a faculty member in the college of engineering at Sana'a University. Unfortunately, in 1994, the civil war started in Yemen and the situation worsened every year. In 1998, with my father's help and the money I had saved, I applied for a Ph.D. program at Syracuse University. The money was enough for one year, but I was hoping some professors in the electrical engineering department may offer me a research assistant scholarship. My first class in my Ph.D. was Wireless Communication with Dr. Varshney and I did well. At the end of the semester, I was lucky again and I was offered a full research assistant scholarship in Dr. Varshney's research lab in image processing and communication, which enabled me to finish my Ph.D. in 2002.

After my Ph.D., I decided to work in the United States where I could continue my cochlear implant research. I went to Yemen twice after graduation and discovered that the politicians there had failed the country and its citizens yet again. I realized that I can help Yemen more from my success in the U.S., starting by donating many textbooks to the electrical engineering department in Sana'a University and sponsoring many senior design projects. In 2003, I gave an expert talk in civil liberties organized by Syracuse University at the second memorial of September 11th. In that talk, which was published in the "Daily Orange," I said, "The attack happened not because Muslims hate America but because for years, the Middle East region has suffered from U.S. foreign policies." That talk received many applauses thanks to Ms. Bermann, who advised me that I could bridge the gap between America and the Middle East by the power of the words instead of violence.

I had the greatest years of my life during my undergraduate study. The education I received made me more confident in my ability to make a difference. My view of America changed to be more positive and the same is true for Ali and Abdu. In America, we were treated as citizens with full rights. We never felt like foreigners because many of our teachers were also Americans with accents like us. I talk about my experience in America with friends and relatives in Yemen. The common thing I hear from them is, "the America you talk about is different from the America that supports dictators in the Middle East and Israel." I tell them the America that I'm talking about is the people I lived with, and not the politicians—America that is governed by a constitution that protects every person living in America regardless of his/her ethnicity, social or immigration status.

I give them an example of how the law protected me from a racist incident that could have ended my dreams when I was on a student visa getting my Ph.D. I was playing with my 5-year-old daughter when I tapped her cheek with the spoon I used to stir my coffee. Unfortunately, it hadn't cooled down enough and ended up leaving a little red mark on her check. The next day at school the teacher reported the mark to the principle and a detective with a social worker came to school and questioned my daughter about the incident. They also questioned the teacher who gave very positive feedback about Saba and her parents. She told the detective that we attend every parental meeting and that she found us to be caring and loving parents and thinks that the incident was an accident. The detective was skeptical and told her that Middle Eastern fathers are always harsh on their daughters. The detective with the social worker and a policeman came to my apartment to interrogate me and my wife. As they were discussing the case in the other room, I heard an argument break out between them after which the detective came out and issued me a ticket for "endangering the welfare of child." As I was staring at the ticket in shock, the social worker handed me her card and told me to contact her if I need her help with the case. I went to the university lawyer who contacted the district attorney who agreed that if I don't make any mistakes for the next 6 months then the ticket will be dismissed but will still remain on my record. The lawyer tried to convince me to accept the offer because if we go to court the jury may view the case the same way the detective saw it which will cost me my scholarship and get me deported from the States. I refused to accept the offer because it was an accident and I had no intent to harm my daughter and furthermore the detective was a racist. At the court scheduling session, the lawyer and I submitted letters from the social worker and my daughter's teacher that supported my parenting and our healthy home environment as well as mentioning the repeated comments the detective made about Middle Eastern fathers. The judge read the two letters and then handed them to the district attorney and told him "I don't think you have a case and don't waste the court's time with cases like these and spend more time with your detective." The district attorney read the letters and agreed, and they dismissed the ticket and sealed the case. This is America that I am talking about. A country with a law that stands by an international student against the city.

Now, I am the Chair of the Engineering and Physics department at the University of Central Oklahoma. Education made me a different person. A math teacher in the middle school in Yemen believed in me and that gave me the confidence to learn and do well. A calculus teacher at Syracuse University, who took the time to talk to me about basketball and the Orangemen, helped me to look at people beyond their appearance and religion. With my accent and imperfect English, Dr. Smith still had confidence in me to offer me a teaching assistant scholarship that enabled me financially to pursue my master's degrees in engineering. A devoted Hindu professor offered me the best research scholarship that enabled me to pursue my Ph.D. Parents tell us the same words of encouragement and believe in us, but we take their words for granted or think parents always think their children are gifted; but when the same words come from a sincere teacher, it makes a huge difference. Education with good teachers changed my perception of people of different colors, races, and religions. College education made me an engineer, but most importantly, made me value humanity and treat people based on their character and not religion or geographic origin. It is easy to fall prey to stereotypes, especially when the traditions we are mocking do not make cultural sense to us. For example, treating a cow like a sacred entity might not make sense to a non-Hindu, while non-Muslims might think it is strange for millions to make a trip to Mecca just to circle a cubical structure, and non-Christians might not understand why they worship a crucified God. In order to conquer our biases, both implicit and explicit, we have to first become aware of them and then actively work to dismantle them by communication and interaction with each other. As a teacher and a chair of the department, I strive to make a difference in the students' lives and perceptions at the University of Central Oklahoma.

> *In order to conquer our biases, both implicit and explicit, we have to first become aware of them and then actively work to dismantle them by communication and interaction with each other.*

I tell my students in the Intro to Engineering class about my experience as a freshman in college and the transition from high school to college. The three messages I try to deliver in this lecture are the power of time management, teamwork, and communication. In high school, we have 10 months to learn the subject, while in college, we have only 3 months and half, so time management is the key to college success. In high school, if I fall back in the first month, I still have 9 months to recover. In college, if you fall back on the first month, then the next two months and half will not be enough to recover. Prioritizing work first and fun second allowed me to dedicate all my focus to learning and enjoying the material and simultaneously reduced the amount of stress clouding my thinking—that transforms a struggle to a success. The second message is communication; if you cannot communicate your ideas, then, similar to a talented dancer dancing in the dark, your ideas will never see the light of day and will die with you. The third message is teamwork. We are not inherently smarter than people were a thousand years ago, however, it was teamwork that enabled humanity to advance from riding horses to visiting the Moon, from taking weeks to deliver a text message in the same continent to delivering speech and video in milliseconds across the word and the universe. Through education for all, communication, and teamwork, humanity was able to accomplish in 150 years what it could not accomplish in thousands of years.

Working in academia may not be financially rewarding like the industry, but the emails I receive from alumni and graduates validate the teachers' noble goal to use their knowledge to help struggling students to discover their strength that has been otherwise stifled by circumstance and social hardship. I even enjoy reading anonymous emails from students thanking me for teaching and telling me that they are praying for me to find my path to the Lord Jesus. I found my path to happiness by being in the classroom, teaching. Even with all of life's twists and turns, my classroom, as always, remains my happy place where I can bring abstract math and science concepts to life by linking theory to practical applications we use regularly in our life. I now understand my 7th grade math teacher's perpetual pride and joy in the classroom.

Education brings peace and prosperity for all humanity. An article published by David Ignatius in the Washington Post on January 27, 2015, mentioned that a recent report for the army, titled, "Assessing Security Cooperation as a Preventive Tool," found that investment in human education is the best way to fight instability in developing countries like Yemen. Education is the cure for poverty, bigotry, and extremism in every society. Because investment in human capital has a large payoff, my dream is to continue teaching at UCO, and starting a foundation that will bring two Yemeni students every year to enroll as undergraduates in the U.S.

MOHAMED BINGABR

Mohamed Bingabr, Ph.D. (Syracuse University) serves as professor of engineering and previously as the Chair of the Engineering and Physics department at UCO. He received several grants for cochlear implant research, has several journal publications in signal processing for cochlear implant and image transmission research, and has a patent in speech strategy for cochlear implants. He has also published five political articles in Yemen to promote democracy and diversity. Bingabr won a faculty merit award for teaching in 2012. In 2013, Bingabr received the Neely Excellence in Teaching award.

PART II

You and Others: Without "We" There is Little Learning

Without personal relationships to stimulate thinking, encourage your journey, or ask new questions, learning can be treacherous. This section offers examples of how others aided and assisted in guiding or sustaining learning journeys.

CHAPTER NINE

Robert Terrell, Ed.D.

How I Learned to Study for Success

A s I sit at my computer contemplating my upcoming retirement in May of 2017, I am reflecting on my teaching career that spans 47 years. Looking back, I realize that I had no intention of becoming a professor of accounting. As a matter of fact, as a freshman in college, I had no idea what an accountant was or exactly what they did.

As a freshman in college, I was very proud of myself sitting in the library reading material for an advanced history class. I must admit that I had no idea what it meant to study for mastery of the material. I believed that if I read the material and marked what I thought were important points, I would be just fine. I am ashamed to admit but these ideas led straight to a "D" in this class. Thank goodness my other grades were a little better and pulled me through.

The next year my future wife (Kathy) enrolled at the university and little did I know what a positive effect she would have on me with regard to my education and choice of career. I started out as a premed student, but after one year of chemistry, I realized this was not my calling. Having one year under my belt, I switched to business and my adviser asked for my major. I had no idea of the options, so I picked accounting because it was first on the list.

I began with Accounting I and promptly failed the first test. Kathy said, "You have got to learn how to study because I do not believe you have a clue." She promptly asked me if I paid attention in class and if I ever wrote notes to emphasize what was important. I responded with a resounding yes and then she pointed out that just because I went to every class did not mean that I was paying close attention. Then she asked if I understood that most people learn through a combination of listening, seeing, and writing. I told her that I had no idea what she meant and then she promptly showed me how this was accomplished. She did inform me that most people learned better with one method than the others but using a combination of all three would be best for the long term. Thanks to her, I was able to increase my study methods and application so that from my sophomore year forward, I was able to make the Dean's list every semester.

There is one more story that must be shared before we can discuss my transformation from poor student to award winning teacher. In my sophomore year, I was required to take a course in speech and debate. Needless to say, I was scared to death at this prospect. However, Kathy again saved my proverbial bacon. As the professor walked in the door and announced that we would each come to the front of the room and present a brief bio, I was ready to bail out of the class. She grabbed me by the arm and said since this is a required course, let's just get it over with. I stayed, and as luck would have it, this course turned out to be one of the best and most meaningful of my educational career. I have spent this part of the chapter trying to show the reader that there are numerous factors, be it personal relationships or situations, that can stimulate and guide us to be thoughtful, creative, and questioning through our educational journey.

After graduating with my bachelor's degree in accounting, I thought I should go back and obtain a master's degree because the marketplace seemed to be demanding more education than just the bachelor's degree. After a year of practice, I applied for graduate school. My alma mater was in need of graduate students to teach part-time while going to school. On the first day of class, I was very nervous, but once I entered the classroom and closed the door, I knew the stage was mine. I was able to teach two years before we purchased a CPA practice of our own in 1972. The practice was very small, so it took some time to build it up. During that period, I realized how much I missed teaching. I opted to apply to teach part-time at a community college and was accepted. In 1974, I was offered a teaching position at the University of Central Oklahoma. From 1976 to 1984, I taught part-time and I returned as a full-time faculty member in January 1985. I can truly say that I have enjoyed every minute I have spent in the classroom working with students.

Kathy and I have published articles and written textbooks, all of which helped me to develop and hone my skills to teach accounting theory and practice. I spent many of my early years teaching subject matter much the same as my instructors did with me. One of the issues in teaching accounting is the volume of material covered in each of the courses. When there is so much material to be covered, it leaves little time to be creative in the classroom. To overcome this problem, I found myself offering tutoring sessions and reviews for tests outside of the limited class time. Granted, this did not allow all students to participate because of their personal and work requirements, but I allowed tape recording of all materials discussed, whether in class or in these outside sessions so the information could be shared.

As fate would have it, after 20 years of practice, Kathy also became a professor of accounting (another story altogether). She and I put together study materials to help students better understand the material and improve their overall performance in the classroom. It became evident to faculty in every discipline that students who are entering college today, and for the last few years, are woefully unprepared for the rigors of college. Many students seem to do well with the basic courses taken in their freshmen and sophomore year, however, a great number falter horribly when faced with the first major course in their chosen field. Admittedly, some students have incorrectly identified the area for which they are best suited. We also see many students, who with the proper training in how to study, encouragement, and the development of their self-worth, become excellent students and go on to a very meaningful and rewarding career in the field of accounting.

> *Students must be aware of the processes and the reasons for various procedures used in the classroom, as well as, outside assignments that may require interpretation, research, analysis and integration.*

From the standpoint of transformational teaching and learning, it is very important for the students to understand what is happening and that they are the major part of the process. Students must be aware of the processes and the reasons for various procedures used in the classroom, as well as, outside assignments that may require interpretation, research, analysis and integration. From the standpoint of several upper level classes that I teach, I have had students work in small groups to solve problems or analyze issues that may arise in the audit of financial statements. In another course at the upper levels, I have students grapple with puzzles and issues in Fraud Examination to help them understand what to look for if they suspect a fraudulent event may be taking place. In the area of financial accounting, students are often asked to work a brief problem in groups so that I may identify students who are having difficulty. Students are very shy in the classroom and often fail to ask questions if they have any. Today's students do not wish to look "foolish" in class. They tend to feel they are the only ones who do not understand the concept, when in reality, many of their classmates are suffering the same fate.

Accounting professors must also teach the students to prepare to enter a profession. In teaching auditing, for example, there is less emphasis on numbers, but a great deal of concern about noting abnormalities. They must also learn to follow guidelines, standards of professional ethics, professional care, and responsibility for upholding the public trust. Students must also be taught that there is not just one right answer in accounting. The Accounting Standards Code is all encompassing and an enormous searchable data base. Teachers in accounting should encourage all students to sit for and pass the Uniform Certified Public Accountants Examination.

Accounting is akin to premed, nursing, dietetics, and engineering. Students must be able to perform to the proper level or they cannot continue. As the students leave our program, they must be able to compete with other students from many different universities for professional jobs requiring certification and licensing. They must be capable of performing as professionals or graduate students. Our university reputation depends upon how the community views the quality of our graduates. We take our responsibility to the community very seriously.

It takes courage to counsel a student who cannot meet the requirements. When I walk into the classroom on the first day of class for Intermediate Financial Accounting I, which requires a grade of B to continue in the program, I have to be honest. I tell them to look around at their classmates because only about 60% will finish the course, and many of those who finish will have a grade of C or below. We do hold extra sessions for additional help and review sessions for upcoming tests. Many students are just not ready for the rigors of this course. We frequently have students who thank us for being honest with them and encouraging them in another field. We always welcome them to come back at a future time if they want to try again. We see many former students who do return and succeed after gaining maturity and confidence.

> *Not only is it important to offer a transformational approach to study and learning in the classroom, but it is equally important to be involved with the students to help aid in their success.*

Not only is it important to offer a transformational approach to study and learning in the classroom, but it is equally important to be involved with the students to help aid in their success. Remembering back to when I was an undergraduate student, it was almost unheard of to speak to your professor outside the classroom. In fact, if you saw them coming down the hallway, students would move over and just nod. One thing I am grateful for today is that students have less fear of their professors and are more than willing to come and see them, ask questions, and often share personal problems or issues.

Students who are willing to open up to their professors should find the college experience to be richer and much more rewarding than those who do not. Speaking for myself, I know that when students open up to me, it provides them a much better learning environment and a college experience that is much more beneficial. I remember with great fondness one of my instructors who always tried to be friendly to me and was very encouraging. While in his classes, I learned a tremendous amount about accounting. Even more, he did an excellent job of modeling for me what a truly gifted and inspiring professor should be. My career has been modeled after this one individual. I have often stated that if I could have the influence on one student's life that this professor had on mine, then my career would have been a success.

I would like to offer some tips that might help others in their learning and teaching journey:

- Prepare students for the level of difficulty of the course.
- Review good study habits with the students in the first week of class or longer if needed.
- Never design a course that will assure everyone an A or B.
- Make eye contact with the students to assess their understanding.
- Encourage students to come and see you if they are having problems in learning or life.
- Enjoy each day in the classroom and be assured that you are making a difference.
- Last, but not least, listen to the students.

I would like to take a moment to thank all those who played such a pivotal role in my accounting career, both as a practicing accountant and a professor of accounting. First and foremost, I want to thank Kathy and my family. My wife had the faith in me and was willing to work even harder than I did to achieve my goals. My sons put up with me working full-time and going to school part-time when I was finishing my doctorate. I would be remiss if I did not acknowledge my professors and colleagues who supported and encouraged all of my efforts. To all of you, I am forever indebted. Finally, I would be remiss if I did not thank each of the many students I have had over the years. Please believe me when I say that you have provided me with more educational experiences in my life than I have ever imparted to you.

ROBERT TERRELL

Robert Terrell, Ed.D. (Oklahoma State University) serves as professor of accounting at the University of Central Oklahoma. He has published textbooks in the areas of financial and managerial accounting, and published articles on fraud accounting and financial accounting. He has won numerous teaching awards, including the Neely Excellence in Teaching award in 2008, Oklahoma Teacher of the Year presented by The Carnegie Institute, Teacher of the Year for the State of Oklahoma presented by the Oklahoma Accounting Society, and Teacher of the Year for the College of Business on two different occasions.

10 CHAPTER TEN

Robert Doan, Ph.D.

It's People That Make the Difference

I t surprised me when I was the recipient. Really surprised me. I'd forgotten that I'd even applied for the Neely Teaching Award. Had only done it at the won't-take-no-for-an-answer request of Mike Knight, Chair of the Psychology Department. If memory serves, he actually told me I had no choice and handed me the outline for the submission.

So, let's start with that interaction and what it meant to me. Why was he so insistent? Did he believe I had a chance to be selected? I couldn't brush it aside and ignore it, I respected him too much, and knew he wouldn't have taken such an action if he didn't believe in me. So, I filled out the necessary information and wrote the essay required by the selection committee. The essay was short, just a few sentences. I decided that I had little chance of actually getting the award and just opted to put my version of teaching truth down on paper. It went something like this: *If you want to be a better teacher, you have to consistently work on becoming a better human being. Better in the sense that you make space for others (students) to be around you in such a manner that they feel better about themselves as a result. Good teaching is the effective use of self that results in positive student self-narrative transformation. It teaches far more than the concepts of a particular academic domain: it teaches important lessons that can be used in the process of making sense of this strange journey on the third rock from the sun. If that occurs, true transformative learning can be witnessed.* If it weren't for the validation and belief of my department chair and friend, I probably would have never written those words. He had done what mentors do; he had believed in me when he didn't have to.

This resulted in my name being called at a university-wide faculty meeting as the recipient of the Neely Teaching Award for 2001. As mentioned above, it surprised me. I was on the verge of quitting teaching, although, I had told no one of this. I won't go into the details of the reasons other than to say it was a considerable state of discouragement about the lack of support for education in Oklahoma. I was actively looking for other ways to make a living. But then my name was called, and I went to the front of the auditorium to accept a warm handshake from Dr. Neely. As he did so, he leaned forward and whispered in my ear, "Best darn essay I ever read."

I felt my eyes moisten but managed to whisper back, "You have no idea how timely this is."

I had just been the recipient of individual transformation caused by the power of an interpersonal validation from someone that matters, someone whose opinion you cannot brush aside. Because of that moment, I sit writing these words in 2016, still a teacher and grateful for it.

But the story goes back further, back to when I was a student in the masters in community counseling program at the University of Central Oklahoma. I had accepted the 'fact' that my education in counseling would end with a masters because I knew I wouldn't be able to pass the statistics classes necessary to obtain a Ph.D. However, Dr. William Frederickson saw it differently and called me into his office one day out of the blue. "I am going to encourage you to get a Ph.D.," he said from behind his large desk. "You're good at being a student, have you considered going on?"

I stirred nervously in my chair and muttered something like, "Uh, I'm no good at stat or experimental design. I couldn't make the B required in those classes."

There is no substitute for good people believing in you. All the technology and computer programs in the world pale in comparison to what happens between people when such an interchange occurs.

"Really?" He leaned forward and put his elbows on the desk. "I'd like to offer you a wager."

"Excuse me," I responded.

"I want you to enroll in my summer section of statistics on an audit basis. You promise to try your best and I promise to grade you harder than anyone else." His eyes twinkled as he spoke. "If you make an A, you apply to some Ph.D. programs next year. If you don't, I won't bug you about it again."

Two subsequent years found me in the Ph.D. in Counseling Psychology Program at the University of Oklahoma where I passed two statistics classes and two experimental design classes. Without the validation of 'Dr. Fred,' I would have never met Dr. Neely on that stage. *There is no substitute for good people believing in you.* All the technology and computer programs in the world pale in comparison to what happens between people when such an interchange occurs. And more, in my opinion, technology can significantly get in the way: it can minimize the human-to-human factor that I believe is necessary for most transformative experiences.

More recently, my interactions with my colleague and friend, Dr. Gabriel Rupp, have proven equally transforming. His support, validation, and consistent understanding of the person I am has seen me through some rough times both professionally and personally. Once again, the validation of an important person has been the key element in my transformation and progress as both a teacher and human being.

This is the bedrock I have built my teaching identity and practice on. I don't use power point presentations, nor am I interested in a classroom where students sit with iPads and answer questions in real time via interacting with a machine. I submit that the most transformative context happens between living people who can look each other in the eyes as they share stories and experiences. I firmly believe that the brain is a narrative instrument that creates meaning out of experience, i.e. it tells stories and makes interpretations in the process of living via making comparisons based on similarity and difference between various ways of being.

> *Transformative learning (is there any other kind?) involves a change in thinking, feeling, and behaving that is maintained long enough to replace an old way of being with a new one.*

The personal transformative experiences I have shared above all involve being presented with an optional point of view of myself by people that I couldn't refute. Two different versions of who I was and what I was capable of achieving. *I have no chance of receiving the Neely Award* versus *someone believes that I can*; *I can't pass statistics* versus *give yourself that chance and see what happens*; and *the best thing I could do is stop teaching* versus *this just may be my calling*. Two distinct versions that I could compare and decide which I preferred.

Transformative learning (is there any other kind?) involves a change in thinking, feeling, and behaving that is maintained long enough to replace an old way of being with a new one. It is not a superficial experience but one that strikes deep into the person's perceptual system and stimulates alteration and difference. It is the difference that actually makes a difference that is observable. It doesn't happen easily and usually requires an experience that goes far beyond instructional directions. I strongly suggest that people don't change because they are told to: they change when it makes sense to them to do so because something has happened that has opened them to the possibility that change is actually achievable. Change occurs when they catch a new view of themselves in the context of enough hope and safety to give it a try. And what sort of change do most humans desire? It almost inevitably involves interacting in a different manner with other human beings; it is most often relational in focus. We aren't teaching hermits; we are teaching a very socially oriented animal. What better way to change relationships than through relationships?

What I attempt to achieve in the classroom is relational and personal and involves engaging the students as unique people who are engaged in the very difficult task of navigating a mortal existence on a planet that is challenging to say the least. It has become more so, rather than less, in the forty plus years I've been teaching. It acknowledges the frustration, anxiety, doubt, and energy that is involved in such a process and the extent of personal toughness and endurance that is required.

I am concerned this is being done less in the higher education context—that a personal validating and confirming relationship with students has gotten lost in the high-tech maze that increasingly is assimilating us. Do we stop to consider, really consider, the difficult world our students live in and how far they have come to sit in our classrooms? I submit that the more this is acknowledged and taken into account during the instructional process, the more productive we will be as teachers. I believe this despite all the rationale I've been hearing lately that today's students are *different* and must be engaged via technology or we will fail to connect. I strongly suggest that just the opposite is true, that in the midst of all the texts, tweets, and emails, that this generation of students is hungry for human connection and understanding, that they are starved for the transforming stimulation of someone who treats them as struggling human beings first, and only secondarily as students. iPhones and computers can't do that. They don't have eyes full of feelings, tone of voice, or nonverbal communication and context. Dr. Neely whispered in my ear, Dr. Fred called me into his office, Dr. Knight took the time to bring me an application, and Dr. Rupp consistently demonstrated his belief in me. None of them used technology in this process: *they used themselves.*

Dr. Neely did that every year at the luncheon those of us lucky enough got to attend. He didn't tell us anything, rather he asked a question about teaching and sat with a notepad recording what we said. He acted as though we had information he could profit from in his own teaching, as if it could transform him. What happens is a two-way flow of information in which both sides can be influenced. We do that for our students and they do it for us if we are present and aware. Transformation that is reciprocal…between people.

That is what counts.

ROBERT DOAN

Dr. Robert Doan is a professor of psychology and a licensed psychologist. He completed the counseling psychology doctoral program at the University of Oklahoma and did his pre-doctoral internship in the Family Therapy Program at the University of Calgary. His primary clinical interest is in the use of narrative therapy and family systems to work with individuals, couples, and families. He also has extensive experience in psychological assessment with youth. In 2001, Doan received the Neely Excellence in Teaching award.

11 CHAPTER ELEVEN

Tawni Holmes, Ph.D., RDN, LD

Don't Burst My Bubble

My Story

M y spouse often says I live in a bubble, and in reflection, this is mostly true. I can see the choices I've made and the people who have led me to this so-called bubble.

As I think about my journey to becoming a professor, there were some key people who inspired me along the way. It wasn't always clear to me what discipline I would teach, but I do remember wanting to be a teacher. Science and health were always the subjects I gravitated towards. My love of learning started with a special teacher in high school and blossomed as I was mentored through my doctoral studies.

My "aha!" moment for becoming a professor was when I realized I wanted to stay immersed in the college experience. I wondered could I really do that?! I knew I couldn't keep getting degrees, but I could certainly teach others and share my passion for learning with students.

Circle of Influence

My parents, Dick and Judy Segress, had the most profound influence on me and the values and principles I live by today, both professionally and personally. They promoted education in our family, and my father often challenged our ideals as a way to stimulate us to think deeply about things. At no point along the way was I discouraged from my goals. I was lucky that I had the opportunities that some do not in that there was never a question whether my brothers or I would go to college—it was an expectation.

While in high school, I was impacted by an influential female role model, Ms. Michelle Maybee. A few of my close friends and I thought we were pretty special because she spent extra time with us letting us talk about life, relationships, and school. As I look back, she wasn't so much trying to be our friend as she was mentoring us to be smart, independent women. Being an engaging teacher, she inspired in me an interest in learning, especially in science, and I believe this was my first inkling that I wanted to be a "cool" teacher too.

As an undergraduate student in college, I discovered my major almost by accident. I was undeclared in the second semester of my sophomore year and was put on notice by advising that I needed to declare a major. At the time, I was taking an Introduction to Nutrition course, and through speaking with the instructor, found out that I could actually major in something I had been interested in for years. Prior to that time, I had never even heard of a dietitian. Opportunities started to come together and my interest in science and health became more than an interest, but a path I wanted to follow.

A very influential figure during my academic career was Mrs. Elizabeth Lohrman. I became her graduate assistant at the Wellness Center where I assisted her in preparing for healthy cooking demonstrations. I learned from her about preparing classes, conducting demonstrations, and the joy of cooking. Elizabeth was instrumental in instilling the idea of "wellness" as an important component of nutrition which would later become my area of emphasis in doing my graduate work.

It wasn't until I was almost finished with my undergraduate degree, and had completed my dietetic internship, that I met my most significant mentor, Dr. Gail Gates (GG). I had the opportunity to spend time with her and discovered that I could do what she did. I could be a scholar and a dietician. Until then, I had never thought that a Registered Dietitian could, in addition to teaching the public about nutrition, be an educator of future practitioners. I could influence what new aspiring dietitians would know. I spent many days in the office of GG. She dedicated so much of her time allowing me to ask questions, make mistakes, and guide me along the way. I learned how to conduct research, and how to teach. I learned from her how to be tough as a professor but be fair in my judgements. Much of how I teach today is influenced by what I learned from her.

So, in this bubble of mine, I along with others, think freely, are passionate and compassionate and are dedicated to pass this possibility on to our students through our teaching.

The "Aha!" Moment

Which brings me back to the bubble. As a student, I remember loving the college experience. I'm not referring to the social events and staying up all night with friends as much as I am referring to the world of open possibilities, the freedom of thought, the idealism, and the constantly changing environment. The idea of studying a topic and your mind being opened to a million more ideas than before. You could change your mind and that was ok. You could test the waters of something, and that was ok too. And once you decided to pursue your passion there was so much to learn that you could never learn it all. So how is this a bubble? The bubble is the world of opportunity where you are shielded in a sense from the outside world. In this bubble, it's ok if everyone is unique and doesn't do or think the same. This is what enriches our experiences and what we thrive upon to make it interesting and to challenge us. In the academia bubble, we encourage and strive for diversity rather than hiding from it.

So, in this bubble of mine, I along with others, think freely, are passionate and compassionate and are dedicated to pass this possibility on to our students through our teaching.

Transformative Teaching and Learning Practice

As a professor in the area of Nutrition, I am dedicated to living a healthy lifestyle and influencing those around me to do the same. I am teaching my students about the science behind why nutrition is so important to overall health so that they can teach others. We talk about promoting health and changing behaviors in the community, and incorporating all aspects of health; mental, emotional, physical, social, environmental, and spiritual. We learn and grow through discussion and debate, and it is a humbling experience at times. In my position, and to those around me, I am looked to as the expert, however, I often feel that I know very little. The realization that there is so much more to learn, and we can never know it all, fuels my understanding of why life-long learning (LLL) has become so much a part of my life.

My philosophy of teaching is to encourage a balance between the student's professional career development and enriching their personal lives. I do so by expecting the student to be collaborators with me in the learning process. For effective learning to take place, an interesting and motivating atmosphere must be provided. To stimulate interest, transformative experiences are implemented, such as service-learning projects, flipping the classroom, team based learning, and multiple ways of accomplishing the same task which allows students to make their own choices. For instance, I might suggest students research a topic and allow them to either write a blog or make a video to support their stance on the issue. Students must take responsibility for actively learning and educators take the responsibility to provide evidence-based information in a clear and unbiased manner. To be a successful learner, the student should not only develop the skills applicable to a specific course, but also learn to apply those skills to practical "real-life" situations, thus developing the whole person.

I continually strive to develop a love of learning and inquiry in my students, which includes the ability to articulate well and listen effectively, often asking them to present material even when it makes them "uncomfortable." I like to think that my influence will enhance their ability to think independently, creatively, and to solve problems. Not only is it important for me to teach them how to ask questions, but also how to find the answers and constantly question what they hear and read. I want their journey to be transformative. I believe learning is most effective when students understand the material

> *Watching them grow from freshman to graduates is inspiring. As I see students maturing, mentoring other students, taking leadership roles, and becoming successful practitioners—this is a sign of success for me.*

yet feel challenged. I find it to be a complement when students find my classes to be "tough." Key components that I try to include in every course I teach are critical thinking, active participation, integrity, leadership, and collaboration.

As a professor, I am allowed to be a student, a teacher, an advisor, and a colleague. I feel a sense of pride in the accomplishments of my students. Watching them grow from freshman to graduates is inspiring. As I see students maturing, mentoring other students, taking leadership roles, and becoming successful practitioners—this is a sign of success for me. I have done my job when I see even a glimmer of that love of life-long learning I hold so significant.

Suggestions for Enhancing Your Learning and Teaching Journey

Often when others find out I have a Ph.D., they mention how smart I must be. I say it is more about *persistence and focus* than it is about intelligence. If you find your passion, follow through, focus on your goals and tune out the chatter around you. All of these suggestions can contribute to a more transformative experience whether teaching or learning:

1. **Be healthy** - in wellness of body and mind. Wellness is the achievement of a person's best in all six components of health; mental, emotional, physical, social, environmental, and spiritual. All components can be affected by the others, if one is weak—it can affect your overall health. Get plenty of sleep, exercise, eat healthy foods, and spend time doing things you love and with people who make you happy. This will translate into your ability to learn and teach others.
2. **Give yourself a break** - Pushing yourself can feel productive and with so many demands and deadlines we tend to overextend ourselves. A lot of LLL's are over-achievers but this can sabotage our health (see 1.) and actually delay our focus and may extend the time it takes to get things done. Find ways to give yourself a break mentally, physically, emotionally, and digitally. You don't have to be on task 100% of the time. As a student, plan your time wisely so that you can include pleasurable activities and allow your mind to reset. As a teacher, give yourself a break!
3. **Give yourself permission to change your mind** - The best answer often changes over time. In many circumstances, changing your mind indicates uncertainty or lack of confidence. Circumstances change, so why does our analysis or focus have to stay static? In academia, as new discoveries are made and as we learn and grow, it's ok to change our mind! As teachers, we change our minds as new information is learned, and as learners, we should be open to those opportunities.

4. **Keep your mind open** - Struggle to stay outside the box, always on the edge, and curious. How else do we continue to learn? Be open to new possibilities, new ways of thinking about something or someone, and the counterargument. Learning takes place when we open our mind to the opinions and possibilities that gives us the realization that we really don't know it all.

5. **Be inspired and inspire others** - The meaning of inspired is "of extraordinary quality, as if arising from some external creative impulse." Be mindful of the creativity that surrounds you so that you may internalize that in a way that helps you become a better you. Instigate it in others by being your best, most creative, and purposeful self. The learning becomes reciprocal.

6. **Look for signs along the way** - The signs may not be obvious but if you are open to the possibilities, they may guide you. At the time, I would not have recognized the signs, but I am confident that by being open to them I was led on this path. I am looking forward to where the signs will take me next and I hope if you're reading this you will look for the signs that may take you on your path to a love of LLL as well!

TAWNI HOLMES

Dr. Tawni Holmes is a Registered Dietitian, professor, and DPD Director in the HES department at UCO where she has been teaching Nutrition/Dietetics since 2004. Prior to coming to UCO, she taught 3 years at San Jose State University in California. She is a native Oklahoman and obtained her degrees at Oklahoma State University. She is a member of the Academy of Nutrition and Dietetics, and the Oklahoma Academy of Nutrition and Dietetics, and serves on the Edmond Mobile Meals Board of Directors. She was awarded the YMCA Service to Youth award in 2012 for an on-going service project related to community gardening. Dr. Holmes was awarded the Vanderford Teaching Award and Neely Excellence in Teaching award in 2014 and nominated for Outstanding Dietetics Educator in 2015. She incorporates many service-learning projects and transformative experiences in her courses and encourages and mentors students to participate in undergraduate research projects.

12 CHAPTER TWELVE

Kaye Sears, Ed.D.

A Growing Passion for Learning About the Family: A Personal Journey

Beginning at a young age, my family constellation changed, and changed several more times. I changed schools a few times as well. Each new experience included a key person that helped me through the transition and encouraged me to be flexible, adaptable, and learn in a "new way." I remember the 4th grade, and at 9-years-old, I moved from a very small oil town in Oklahoma to a very large school in Dallas, Texas. It was a daunting experience to recall walking to school with my sister and brother and getting lost a few times on the way home. After half of a school year, it was back to the small town and a relief to be back home, only, I would soon move to another small town. After a couple of years in one place, half-way through my senior year I moved to a very large metropolitan school. This was probably one of the most critical times for me as I moved out of my small school comfort zone, where I was in a leadership position in my senior class, and landed in a very large school system where the senior class was almost as large as my former high school. I survived that experience and was able to graduate with the help of a very kind coach who helped me every day to find classes, meet a few people, and survive until I graduated. All along the way, it was a special person in all the schools that made the transitions manageable for me and made the difference in how I perceived the school and my experiences. The teachers took an interest in me, encouraged me, and invested in me with their time and friendship. These experiences that transformed me also showed me how I could be "that special person" to other students, as I would realize later, offer transformative learning experiences to them.

Higher Education Journey

Without being aware of the impact of my experiences at the time, I was developing a clear interest and passion to learn about the family and how it influences members on so many levels. I was the first one in my family to pursue a higher education degree, and was not necessarily encouraged to go, but it seemed to be a choice. The fact that I lived in a college town, I just assumed I would go to the University of Oklahoma. I thought it would be fun, but at the time, had no aspirations to go further than the B.S. that I signed up to complete. As I pursued my Bachelor of Science in Home Economics, I was excited to be on the famous football championship team campus (16,000 students) and to have chosen a major that taught me so much about myself and others, was able to make friends with like interests, and feel like that was where I belonged at the time. In the beginning of my college experience, I chose my major of Home Economics because of the influence of a former teacher in one of those small towns, and because of the emphasis on the family. I wanted to learn about how the family developed and coped during the many stages of the life cycle, additions and subtractions, changes, interruptions, crises, and their uniqueness. Then I would know how to help them through education and intervention in the future, and to make a difference. I found out I really liked school, learning, being a part of a college campus culture, and meeting a lot of new people. This was a huge change for me to go from the very shy schoolgirl I was for so many years through public school, to someone that slowly became more engaged in the learning process at a different level with some ideas of my own to share. The process of being transformed by my experiences are important for me to share with students about how important the family is to each member and society as a whole.

The process of being transformed by my experiences are important for me to share with students about how important the family is to each member and society as a whole.

Travel: A Ticket to Other Cultures

A few years and two children later, I began a master's degree in education at the University of Central Oklahoma (called Central State University at the time). The areas of focus for me were the development of children and an interest in nutrition for children. I also was the co-director of a summer camp for underprivileged children from 1960–1969. In 1969, I received my M.Ed. from Central State University and we welcomed a 3rd child. These experiences prepared me to work with the Kickapoo Head Start Training Center in Jones and McCloud, Oklahoma, as a Parent Educator and Nutrition consultant for the children in that Head Start program from 1965–1972. The families were accepting, eager to work with me, invited me to their homes, and gave me insight into their family structure. During several years with them, I also began teaching adjunct at Central State University in 1972 and working with the State Health Department Maternal and Child Health Division. These jobs gave me an opportunity to teach child nutrition in the six-state region of Head Start and a chance to participate in training on Pueblos in Santé Fe, New Mexico, which opened up a new population of families for me to teach, learn from, and observe.

This opportunity to work with the people in New Mexico was one of the life experiences that moved me toward my interest in other cultures, the study of families, and my need to interact with the families in other countries. I now look back on my personal journey and see that it is clear I have been headed in the same direction for years. I learned by listening, spending time with mentors, studying and learning from personal experiences interacting with families in many of the 27 different countries I have visited.

I have been truly transformed as I became acquainted with families across cultures. Through all of these earlier years of working with families in various roles, my interest increased for learning about families, gaining more experiences with them, and looking at similarities and differences among cultures. During the 1980s, every 2 years, another colleague and I took students on international trips where we visited schools, the Montessori headquarters, government agencies, families in their homes, and listened to social service discussions as well. An opportunity to observe families in France, Italy, England, Wales, Scotland, and Ireland was a chance to see them in their own country, visit with them, and observe them with their families.

During the 1990's I was privileged to visit homes of families in Russia, Alaska, Canada, and Africa, and to also observe families in Greece and Turkey as well. Each experience exposed me to cultural differences among families in these various countries, but also, I saw evidence of the similarities that were so poignant to me. An example of one similarity was the love and care the parents showed for their children, the involvement of the fathers with their children, and the intergenerational interactions in many of the countries. The practice of young adults living at home until they marry was also a common practice among many cultures. Parents were also very involved in their young children's schools.

As I began this part of my journey, I got an opportunity to develop leadership skills by participating on the team that brought two professional organizations to the Oklahoma City area. In 1974, I was one of a small group of professionals in the field of early childhood education and development that organized the Oklahoma chapter of the National Association for the Education of Young Children (OKAEYC) out of a need to provide leadership for training and support for our professionals and paraprofessionals in the field. Another purpose was to improve the quality of programs for our Oklahoma children in full day childcare. I became the first president of the organization and am still a member today. In the 1970s, I was, again, part of a small group that also included three Oklahoma State University professors who met one icy day at one of the professor's homes to organize the Oklahoma chapter of the National Council on Family Relations (OkCFR). I am still a member of this organization and have served on the board since the 70s. The student affiliates of both organizations at UCO in the Human Environmental Sciences Department provide great opportunities for students to get leadership experiences, a chance to meet students of like interests, and to attend and present at the national conferences.

A Favorite: Teaching in Higher Education

I loved teaching and knew that I wanted to teach at Central State University. That meant a doctorate was necessary, so, in 1975, I was hired fulltime and later that school year was admitted to the doctoral program at Oklahoma State University and began that journey. I was closing in on the completion of this goal, but getting tired with 3 children, a fulltime job and a doctoral program (and no computer). Just in time, another positive incentive was the encouragement I needed to go the extra mile. I was given a $200 scholarship from my department at OSU. If they cared about my success and supported me, I could do it. I completed my doctorate in August 1978 and completed the requirements to become a licensed Marriage and Family Therapist, and a Clinical member of the American Association of Marriage and Family Therapy.

A favorite course to teach was one about family, which included the assignment of a genogram. This assignment was a transforming experience for most of the students. It was an invaluable experience for the students who often made family connections with members they didn't know, reconnections with grandparents, and other members through email. Some students helped family members mend family estrangements that had persisted through many years. The students loved their finished products and often gave a copy of it as a gift to all members of their family. This assignment was a transformative learning experience for me, as well as the students, as they told stories of how this had impacted them and their families. In 2007, I had to give that class to a very competent adjunct faculty member who had taken the course from me as an undergraduate major. I became department chair for Human

Environmental Sciences. This new assignment and role may have been, and continues to be, one of the most interesting and enjoyable transformative learning experiences in recent years. I feel blessed that I get to advise the graduate students along their educational story that is transformative for both of us. I am grateful to get to work with faculty and staff around the campus that mentor for me regularly.

I know a student's environment affects their ability and willingness to learn, so I try to provide a "user friendly" environment where all students are challenged in a supportive atmosphere and they want to learn. Human dignity and diversity must be respected in everything we teach and model. It is fun for students to have class discussions, and also to work in groups, because it gives students an opportunity to get acquainted, and learn from one another. I regularly use this technique in the classes I teach and find they are valuable tools. A part of my responsibility to each student as they attend our university is not only while they attend classes, but when they graduate and enter the field.

> *I know a student's environment affects their ability and willingness to learn, so I try to provide a "user friendly" environment where all students are challenged in a supportive atmosphere and they want to learn. Human dignity and diversity must be respected in everything we teach and model.*

As I look back on my trip from then to now, it is clear that I have been on a track to learn more, care more, and to continue teaching and sharing more about families. I remember the college students through the past four decades with interesting hair styles and colors, often braless and shoeless, many styles of dress, makeup, no makeup and class interaction styles. The years have taught me so much. My way of thinking, teaching and working with students have changed from a young and new faculty member on the campus of Central State University, and I continue to change with each new group of students.

Clearly my interactions with families through the years have given me opportunity to create excitement and interest in students to learn about family dynamics. Each time I welcome a new class, greet a new major, advise students about courses and jobs, help them find the wonderful resources at UCO for those who need help, listen to them about their needs, wants, interests, bad news, good news, and exciting news, I have learned something new. It has been fun, and continues to be, when students and alumni bring their babies and pets for me to meet. It is such a proud feeling when I see the alumni attending meetings, presenting, speaking, and making a difference where they are working.

I am Now What I Wanted to Be Then

I am a product of many experiences, events, special teacher mentors, my student mentors, and my own family scenarios. I am finishing my 44th year on this campus; I have transitioned through three name changes, and five wonderful presidents. I am on my third generation of some families in the Child Study Center Laboratory where our students study children through play. I work with three faculty and two staff on my team in the HES family that went through "my" undergraduate and graduate programs. They have now been teaching students in Family Life Education for more than two decades and are transforming lives of students as well. This is where I love to serve and can't think of anything else I'd rather do.

KAYE SEARS

Kaye Sears, Ed.D. serves as a professor of environmental studies and Academic Coordinator for Graduate Studies at the University of Central Oklahoma. She has served as Department Chair since 2007 and has been teaching at UCO for over 40 years. Some of her numerous awards include the Neely Excellence in Teaching Award in 2002, Vanderford Distinguished Teacher Award in 2007, Luminary Society 2015, Modeling the Way 2013, Senior Faculty Award for Professional Contributions 2012, Distinguished Achievement Award from Oklahoma Council on Family Relations in 2013, and most recently, the Certified Family Life Educator National Special Recognition Award in 2015.

13 CHAPTER THIRTEEN

Matthew Hollrah, Ph.D.

The Man from Borneo and the Consummate Explainer

I have often wondered how much my family background has contributed to my becoming a teacher. In some ways, it should be obvious to me. I was born into a family full of educators. My father was an earth science and biology teacher. My maternal grandfather was a teacher and a football coach. His son, my uncle, was a football coach, a high school principal, and an English teacher. My grandmother was a school nurse, and my aunt is a school librarian. Two of my mother's cousins are professors in the U.K., so, you could say that I simply went into the family business, but that answer has never fully satisfied me. Just as many of us didn't become teachers.

Another possible explanation is that my mother became pregnant with me while she was finishing her bachelor's degree in elementary education. She struggled for a time with the decision to finish the degree or not. I was a more immediate and demanding responsibility. However, she ultimately decided she was too close not to finish, and briefly put me in daycare while she went to class. She would drive down Washington St. in Stillwater, OK, look north up the street, and say to me, "There's Matthew's big building" before she dropped me off. This is perhaps not insignificant. At the age of two or three, my mother declared that the biggest library for miles around belonged to me. Did I really know what that building was, what it meant? Maybe not. But I can say that, technically, the first class I ever attended was not kindergarten or even pre-school but a college course likely on some aspect of education.

More likely, though, my interest in teaching comes directly from my parents. My father was by all accounts a fantastic science teacher. Before the phrases "student-centered classroom" or "inquiry-based learning" ever entered the lexicon of educational theorists, this is what my father was doing. In fact, his high school assistant principal, who had visited his classroom on several occasions, once said to him, "Bob, I know you are a good teacher, but I never see you teach." What he saw instead was a classroom full of activity because students were doing experiments, using equipment, and generally trying to find things out. If teaching meant lecturing, then that assistant principal surely didn't see my father teach.

At home, Dad was the consummate explainer. He never missed a chance to show me how something worked. If he was about to mow the yard, he'd show me how the lawnmower worked. If he was planting seeds in the garden, he'd explain how to condition the soil and water them in. He knew the name of every tree and seemingly of every bird and bug that flew or crawled by. He'd let me play with his tools, hammer nails, saw wood. His teaching was a teaching by explaining but also by doing.

My mother's approach was different. I guess I was a curious child, and while she did the dishes or cooked or performed any number of other tedious household tasks, I would pull a little, wooden, green chair into the kitchen, sit down on it, and fire off a million questions. One day, probably after I had asked all the questions she cared to answer, my mother took a different approach and really "flipped the classroom." She became the Man from Borneo.

The Man from Borneo spoke with an accent. In my memory, it is vaguely Slavic. Mom never was any good with geography, but she knew that Borneo was far away and had a certain exotic ring to it. Having recently arrived in Oklahoma and our kitchen, the Man from Borneo didn't know how to do the simplest of things. It then became my job to tell him how to do them. Only years later when I started teaching myself did I realized what a clever trick this is. I use it regularly by pretending like I don't understand a reading or a key concept in order to get my students to explain it to me. And it works without the accent. We all know that if you teach something, you learn it even better. That is what my mother was doing. Instead of me asking a question and she answering it, she asked the questions, and I had to give the answers.

The Man from Borneo would say, "I no understand how to wash plate. Tell me how to wash plate." I would then have to tell him the exact steps of washing a plate. This process was further complicated by the fact that he would take certain things I said literally. So if I said, "First, pick up the plate," he would hold the plate high in the air or hold it tightly with two hands straight out in front of him. Then I would laugh and say, "Mom, not like that," to which she would reply, "I not Mom. I Man from Borneo." Sometimes the game would happen in the car on the way to the store. The Man from Borneo would say, "I not know how to get to store. How I get to store?" The conversation would turn into something like the Abbot and Costello "Who's on First?" skit. "Turn left," I would say. He would ask, "Left?" I would say, "Right." "Okay, I turn right," he would say, and he would start turning right instead of left to which I would say, "No, no! Turn left!"

So many things were happening in these moments that I only now understand. I do not know if my mother was drawing upon something she learned in an education course or if she just naturally had incredible instincts about, and insights into, how kids learn. Regardless, I was discovering all sorts of things simultaneously about language. I was learning how to be specific with language by giving all the steps to a process. I was learning how to explain things in terms that someone unfamiliar with my daily life would understand. And I was learning that words have more than one meaning. In fact, in talking to my mother more recently about these moments, my surprise and realization at the multiple meanings of words was for her the best part of the game. As a learner, I didn't even know I was learning these things until much later. However, I've come to see that what we often call "student engagement" looks a lot like this kind of immersive learning experience in which students almost forget that they are in class.

From the teacher's perspective, I try to design activities that help students creatively engage with simulated problems—i.e., a kind of game, but one that isn't necessarily competitive. The Man from Borneo asked me questions to which I generally already knew the answers. However, the answers to his questions didn't always produce the desired result, e.g., turning right instead of left. I then had to rethink my answer and phrase it in a way to produce the desired result. This was, in essence, a fun way to get me to reflect on what I was doing, and in the past fifteen years or so, educational research in the teaching of writing has started to pay more attention to reflection as an important part of the learning process. I could have gotten mad about the fact that the Man from Borneo didn't understand what I thought was a perfectly good answer, but instead, it was fun because his reactions were fun and funny.

In the teaching of writing, too, sometimes I think that my primary goal is to get students to write sentences that they didn't know they would write—to surprise themselves.

As we get older, this kind of play-learning might seem childish, but what is the essential difference in this kind of learning and what happens when an experiment produces a problematic but informative result? In the teaching of writing, too, sometimes I think that my primary goal is to get students to write sentences that they didn't know they would write—to surprise themselves. And those surprises often come at my Man-from-Borneo-like prompting. "This is an interesting idea," I might say to a student, "what were you driving at here?" This prompt is not exactly like pretending not to know how to wash a plate, but more often than not, I know what the student meant to say. I just want him or her to figure out a better, clearer, or more analytic way to write by reacting to their writing as if I, the reader, don't quite understand what they meant.

At the same time, it was just as important for me as a learner to be able to reflect on different ways of achieving the desired end as I was in the process of trying to reach that end. Built into the immersive experience was an element of reflection—what we might call metacognition—without which I wouldn't have been aware of the need to experiment, and ultimately, to think critically and creatively. Much later, I would be able to reflect separately and more thoroughly on this learning process. But building reflection into the immersive experience itself seems to make the experience all the more immersive.

To be the Man from Borneo, my mother had to know how to improvise, which isn't a bad term to assign to these quick reflections that happen in the midst of the immersive experience that I've been trying to describe. We often think of reflection as being what one does after an immersive experience. And, obviously, one can do this. But to improvise, one has to reflect quickly in the process of doing in order to achieve some desired end. Improvisation in this richer sense is somewhat ignored as an aspect of effective teaching. The old model of teaching, the model that Paolo Freire has famously called the "banking model" of education, requires little to no improvisation. In this traditional model, the teacher plans a lecture or presentation. That lecture is full of information that the teacher believes students need to know. The students listen, take notes, and supposedly absorb the information. Freire[1] puts it this way, "Education thus becomes an act of depositing, in which the students are the depositories and the teacher is the depositor. Instead of communicating, the teacher issues communiqués and makes deposits which the students patiently receive, memorize, and repeat" (p. 72). With students as bank accounts into which teachers deposit "knowledge," what need is there for improvisation? Of course, we are learning how ineffective this "banking" approach to teaching truly is. But in learning this, we are also finding out that more effective teaching requires a different set of skills than perhaps we thought were necessary, and some of them, like improvisation, are difficult, though not impossible, to teach.

For a long time, I thought I learned improvisation from listening to jazz. In the bebop tradition, musicians start with a "standard," or a pop song that most audience members will know. The band begins by playing "the head," which is the part of the song that the audience immediately recognizes. Shortly after the head, the band hits "the break," which literally breaks with the traditional way the song has been played to allow for improvisation, which usually changes up the melody and defamiliarizes the song. This model of creative group interaction is part of what I'm trying to do in the classroom, especially when I'm trying to figure out which questions will provoke students into good discussion. Once I've gotten a student or two to respond, then I can take their responses and run with them, spinning off new questions or maybe even an impromptu activity that has used the ideas they have come up with in that class discussion. Experienced listeners of jazz will hear this phenomenon happening in the way the band members interact. The band leader, usually a trumpet or saxophone, will start the break, and then the other members of the band will respond in turn. Eventually, the leader comes back in and offers his response to their solos. It's dialogical improvisation, taking a standard or predetermined idea and seeing where you can take it in the course of a few minutes.

> *Once I've gotten a student or two to respond, then I can take their responses and run with them, spinning off new questions or maybe even an impromptu activity that has used the ideas they have come up with in that class discussion.*

I should stress, though, that in order to improvise well, I need to have a base to work from. When I walk into a classroom, I always have an outline or set of notes about where I want the class to go, and this outline is, of course, tied to a reading or writing assignment we are working on that week. Often, I use a five-part structure to organize the class period, but my outline of this structure implies a linearity that almost never happens. I move in and out of these parts of the structure mostly in response to what the class seems to need or want. An oversimplification of the process goes like this. First, I introduce a concept or idea that is related to a reading, making sure that everyone in the class understands the concept or has the opportunity to ask a question about it. Perhaps this is the analogue of "the head" I mentioned earlier. Second, I model one way to think analytically about the idea or a way to apply the abstract concept in practice. Maybe this is me acting as the band leader who gets the privilege of the first solo. Third, I let the class loose in little quartets of their own to try out their ways of applying the concept. But they can't do it just like I did it because I give them some kind of tough question to answer, one similar in difficulty to a hard, short-answer test question. If it isn't a challenge, then they don't have a reason to push themselves into creative and interesting improvisations. Fourth, we bring the ways the students applied the concept in their small groups into dialogue with one another. We get to hear the back and forth of the groups' ideas in relationship to the main one that kicked everything off. Finally, we come back to the original concept, a kind of coda, in order to make sure students don't forget the purpose of our improvisations.

I have to admit that some class periods sound and feel a lot more coherent than others. Sometimes, not nearly enough, my classes feel like the Miles Davis Quintet, and at least once a semester, I'm that lonely piano player in the hotel lobby with a single dollar in the tip jar. More often than not, though, this jazz-like method, creates a classroom that takes students' ideas seriously and establishes high expectations for class participation. It makes students think, and it asks students to collaborate in their thinking. And even though I'm clearly the leader, I am inquiring and interpreting and improvising and collaborating with my students in order to make sense of whatever it is that we happen to be studying.

In reflecting on how my parents influenced my understanding of teaching, I've created an implied binary between my father's and mother's kinds of teaching that is in some ways false and reductive. Dad's way of teaching draws upon aspects of Mom's and vice versa. But that is exactly the point. Within the improvisation required by the Man from Borneo is a knowledge of how things work. I have to know my discipline to be able to improvise questions and approaches to learning it. At the same time, being a good explainer and helping students learn-by-doing requires one to improvise—to know how to think on one's feet, to adapt to an unexpected moment. When a student comes up with a surprising answer to a question, or when no one speaks at all, I have to figure out in the moment what to do, which sends me right back to my repertoire of teaching tricks and disciplinary concepts. I had thought for some time that it was jazz that taught me how to do this, but I see now that jazz was the metaphor that helped me understand that I have been merging my parents' approaches so that the Man from Borneo and the consummate explainer fuse to become a new character, a band leader whose job it is to guide students in a particular direction based on what we need to learn but also to follow where the students take me when they "get it."

MATTHEW HOLLRAH

Dr. Matthew Hollrah is a Professor of English and the Chair of the English Department at UCO. He is a native of Stillwater, Oklahoma, where he received his B.A. in English from Oklahoma State University. He also holds an M.F.A. in Creative Writing (poetry) from Western Michigan University and a Ph.D. in English from the University of Kansas. Dr. Hollrah's scholarly work has appeared in the *minnesota review*, *READER*, and the edited collection *Authorship Contested: Cultural Challenges to the Authentic, Autonomous Author*. He is also the author of two online composition textbooks published by Great River Learning entitled *So What?* and *Now What?* His poetry has been published in the *Swansea Review*, *Soundings Review*, *This Land*, and the anthology *Ain't Nobody That Can Sing Like Me: New Oklahoma Writing*. In 2014, Hollrah received the Neely Excellence in Teaching award.

14 CHAPTER FOURTEEN

Christy Vincent, Ph.D.

Learning is the Thing for You

Introduction

I n T.H. White's *The Once and Future King*, Merlyn advised the young King Arthur: *"The best thing for being sad is to learn something. That's the only thing that never fails."* The statement resonates with my life experience. I love to learn. Always have. I love to teach as well. It was the only thing I played as a child—school. Yes, I played school. Armed with the roll book and small chalkboard my mother bought for me at the local bookstore, my bedroom became a school room for all of my stuffed animals and dolls. Pleased that our old house had roller blinds on the windows, I created my lessons on the chalkboard and then hid the board behind the blind. I brought in my "students," called roll, and with great exuberance and purpose, raised the blind to show them the day's lesson. *They* may not have learned anything, but in order for me to teach, *I* had to *learn*. I had so much fun.

I still think learning is fun. Conversely, navigating through the rigors of my undergraduate and graduate programs was sometimes anything *but* fun. I faced multiple obstacles as I worked a job, maintained a household, cared for my children, helped my aging parents, and kept up relationships with friends and extended family. Any one of these obstacles could have derailed me and kept me from completing my degrees. These experiences remind us that learning occurs in the midst of a *life*—and life events can sometimes threaten the basic sense of wellness and health required for learning to take place.

According to Silverman, Underhile, and Keeling,[1] student health is a critical foundation for learning. They state, "Health creates *capacity*; students whose health status is positive and flourishing have greater ability and readiness to learn and engage fully in all meaningful educational experiences." Additionally, they define student health broadly as "the reflection of the state of *physical*, *emotional*, *psychological*, and *social* well-being that constantly…affects student learning" (p. 7). Being unwell in any of these areas can keep individuals from learning. Recalling my university experiences, I can name several critical moments in which my basic sense of wellness in one or more of these categories was threatened. In those times, I was fortunate to receive some form of *social support*,[2] and that support was the difference between me succeeding or failing.

In this essay, I will explore a specific critical moment in my learning journey when others provided social support to help me. I will discuss how this support shaped my perspective as a professor and prepared me to take an active role in supporting student health and wellness on my campus. Finally, I will provide suggestions for both giving and receiving social support with the aim of helping students maintain a basic sense of wellness and health vital to their learning journeys.

A Critical Moment in My Learning Journey

Unlike many of my peers, I did not receive my doctorate degree until I was 41 years old. I went to graduate school immediately after completing my bachelor's degree. In the gap between the completion of my master's degree and my entrance to a doctoral program, I lived a life away from academia, working for a small entrepreneurial company in sales and marketing. In fact, during that portion of my life, I thought that my career as a teacher was over. At age 35, along with a change in life circumstances, came the opportunity to work toward my doctorate. I taught 15 hours per semester as a graduate assistant or adjunct professor (at three different universities) while working on my doctorate.

After completing my course work and preparing to write my prospectus and collect data for my dissertation, I became pregnant at age 39. In week 20 of the pregnancy, I was shocked to discover that there were *two* babies in my womb—twins. In week 31 of the pregnancy, I met with my doctoral committee and defended my prospectus. That was a Friday in April. The identical twin baby boys arrived eight weeks prematurely the following Wednesday. Because my adjunct teaching responsibilities continued until May, I went back and forth between the university and the Intensive Care Unit as the babies' bodies grew strong enough to leave the incubators. I managed to wrap up the Spring semester at the university about the time the babies were cleared to come home.

The first year of their lives is a blur to me. As I enjoyed caring for them, I was also somewhat haunted by the unexamined, unanalyzed data from my dissertation begging for attention from the drawers of my filing cabinet. I had come so far in my journey toward a doctorate, I was determined not to let life circumstances keep me from completing my dissertation. Nevertheless, my little squirmy, crying, cooing "life circumstances" managed to take all of my attention. About that time, I found out that I would *not* have an adjunct contract in the Fall semester. Those were trying times. No job, no dissertation, no breaks, not enough money, not enough sleep.

That November, I was offered an opportunity to give a presentation at a lunch meeting of the local chapter of the Society for Human Resource Management (SHRM). My area of expertise and the subject of my not-yet-written dissertation was conflict management. My tips for managing conflict in the workplace were printed on a handout I distributed during my presentation. So was my contact information. The following day, I received a call from the director of Human Resources at a local, large health system. She had heard my presentation and wanted to talk to me about a job opportunity as an Organizational Effectiveness consultant. I was very interested in the job and was certain that if I took it, I would not finish my dissertation. When I discussed my concerns, the director offered to hire me and allow me to work part-time until I completed my dissertation—at a rate of pay that was many times what I had been making as an adjunct. Until this day, I refer to that fateful presentation for SHRM as a "miracle." By the way, this director rarely had time to attend SHRM meetings. She saw the announcement about a guest presentation on conflict management and decided to go on *that* day.

A few weeks later, on January 2nd, I left the now eight-month-old twins with a sitter and began working about 20-30 hours per week in the HR Department. The money I made allowed me to hire a sitter for the days I was not working in HR so that I could write my dissertation. I completed the dissertation in August, was awarded my Ph.D., and began working full-time for the director after that. While I enjoyed the years I worked at the health system, I missed academia. I missed teaching. Five years later, when the boys were ready to start Kindergarten, I applied for, and was offered a tenure-track position in the Mass Communication Department at the University of Central Oklahoma (UCO). Getting back into academia would have been impossible if I had not been afforded the opportunity to complete my dissertation earlier. That gift—that incredible arrangement of well-paid, part-time work was a type of social support that allowed me to succeed—and it changed my life.

Social Support, Wellness and Transformative Learning

House's model of social support describes four types of support that people who are in interpersonal relationships can offer to each other—emotional, instrumental, informational, and appraisal. Social support concerns the question: "*Who* gives *what* to *whom* regarding *which* problems?" (p. 22). House[3] defines the different types of support as follows:

- *Emotional Support* involves demonstrating care, concern, trust, empathy, or love.
- *Instrumental Support* involves providing direct aid such as money, time, or assistance.
- *Informational Support* involves providing information that people can use to help themselves.
- *Appraisal Support* involves providing feedback or affirmation for self-evaluation purposes.

I received all of these forms of social support during this critical moment in my learning journey; however, what should seem clear from the details of my story is that the *instrumental support* I received from the director was vital to my success. I received other instrumental support during this time in the form of meals delivered to my home, provision of a quiet space for me to work, and someone coming to clean my house on occasion. This form of social support aided with all aspects of my health and wellness and provided an environment supportive to my learning. Receiving instrumental support in addition to the other forms helped me on the journey that culminated in my graduate degree. My appreciation for this support has shaped my view of my role as a professor and member of the university community. I understand from my own experiences the importance of health and wellness to the learning process and the importance of *social support* to a basic sense of health and wellness.

> *I understand from my own experiences the importance of health and wellness to the learning process and the importance of social support to a basic sense of health and wellness.*

My anecdotal experiences have been confirmed in research studies. Cohen, Underwood, & Gottlieb[4] cite numerous studies that illustrate the relationship between social support and health and wellness. This is particularly true with an expanded view of health to include *physical, emotional, psychological,* and *social* health.[5] Further, many scholars have found a relationship between perceived social support and a number of variables related to undergraduate student success, satisfaction, well-being, and persistence.[6]

In 2004, the National Association of Student Personnel Administrators (NASPA) and the American College Personnel Association (ACPA)[7] called for an "integrated use of all of higher education's resources in the education and preparation of the *whole* student," and introduced "new ways of understanding and supporting learning and development as intertwined, inseparable elements of the student experience." They advocated for "transformative education—a holistic process of learning that places the student at the center of the learning experience" (p. 1). They critiqued universities' approach to learning by stating:

> Clearly, learning is far more rich and complicated than some of our predecessors realized when they distinguished and separated learning from student life. Seeing students as their component parts (body, mind, spirit), rather than as an integrated whole, supported the emergence of fragmented college systems and structures—academic affairs to cultivate the intellect, and student affairs to tend the body, emotions, and spirit. (p. 3)

About that same time, UCO began emphasizing a form of transformative education that encourages high-impact teaching practices, calls for an *integration* of the students' curricular and co-curricular experiences, and encourages students to develop beyond-disciplinary skills in the areas of:

- Leadership,
- Service Learning and Civic Engagement,
- Research, Creative and Scholarly activities
- Global and Cultural Competencies, and
- Health and Wellness.

Over the past decade or so, this Transformative Learning initiative has allowed the university to receive several grants to support the practices that help first generation college students and other at-risk students (who may not have all types of social support) to persist in their academic journeys. The grants have also placed UCO among leaders in the country in developing a mechanism to capture these transformative curricular and co-curricular learning experiences in a record—the Student Transformative Learning Record (STLR). The students' STLR reports along with their academic transcripts allow them to demonstrate their competencies to employers and graduate school admissions officers.

The inclusion of *health and wellness* as one of the Transformative Learning tenets illustrates the university's commitment to supporting one of the most, if not the most, important factor in student learning. To support students' health and wellness, the university provides significant resources in the form of student services, programming, facilities, and personnel. As a vocal supporter of an expanded definition of health and wellness and an advocate for the significance of wellness in students' capacity to learn, I was chosen to serve as the *Faculty Liaison for the Health and Wellness Transformative Learning Tenet* at our university for a number of years. As such, I helped faculty to support students' health and wellness in a number of ways. One way faculty can help is to provide social support to students in an effort to contribute to their *overall* health and sense of well-being.

Offering and Accepting Social Support

Faculty members are in a prime position to offer several forms of social support. In many campuses, but particularly in commuter universities, professors and instructors are the "face" of the university. Students drive to school, park their cars, go to their classes, and then leave the university. They may not be aware of the numerous support services available to students, but they do interact with their professors. Furthermore, professors are in the ideal place to witness problems that students may be having in one or more aspects of their health and wellness. As such, professors can be the connectors between students and the support services available. This requires professors to be aware of these services, but more importantly, it requires professors to *see this as their role*. In this way, the professor can provide *informational* support that contributes to the students' wellness and perhaps their capacity for learning. In Zavatkay's[8] research on social support, students placed a *higher value* on *informational* support from their *professors* over that of *emotional* support from their family members and a close friend. The information can be about the course or study skills. It can also be about the services the university offers to help students maintain their health.

> *We all can remain aware that students are learning in the midst of a life—a life that can detract from the basic sense of health and wellness that is needed for learning to take place.*

Faculty members may offer *appraisal* support by giving frequent, constructive feedback on their assignments. Zavatlay's study found that the more social support students perceived from professors, the more likely the students were to persist. Instructors may offer *emotional* support in the form of faculty mentoring. Faculty members may not be in the position to offer tangible aid or *instrumental* support; however, they can contribute to that support through a willingness to write recommendation letters for students seeking tuition waivers and other forms of financial support from the university.

Faculty members, I encourage you to consider the relationship between your students' health and wellness, their capacity for learning, and their academic success. We all can remain aware that students are learning in the midst of a *life*—a life that can detract from the basic sense of health and wellness that is needed for learning to take place. We can recognize that in critical moments of the learning journey, an amount of social support in one form or another can make the difference between students' success and failure. In addition to facilitating students' learning of the content of your discipline, please also facilitate the students' awareness of the university resources to support their health and wellness.

For those readers who are currently in college, I encourage you to consider the importance of your health and wellness to your capacity to learn. Take action to manage your stress. Attend to your physical, emotional, psychological and social health. Seek all forms of social support to contribute to your overall sense of health and well-being. Recognize that those who have taken this journey before you have also faced critical moments during which their success depended on the support they received from others. Take advantage of the numerous services offered on campus to support you. Finally, I encourage you not to confuse the navigation of the formal educational system (e.g., getting a degree) with engagement in lifelong learning. The system is meant to support you and to provide objective evidence of your learning. Nevertheless, getting through the system can sometimes detract from the joy of learning for learning's sake. Try to keep this from happening. As T.H. White's Merlyn said to King Arthur, *"Learning is the only thing which the mind can never exhaust, never alienate, never be tortured by, never fear or distrust and never dream of regretting. Learning is the thing for you."*

CHRISTY VINCENT

Dr. Christy Vincent is a Professor in the Mass Communication Department at the University of Central Oklahoma where she teaches organizational and strategic communication courses. Her research interests include conflict management, mediation, change management, executive coaching, and training and development. Her interest in conflict management led her to the Straus Institute for Dispute Resolution at the Pepperdine University School of Law where she earned a Certificate in Alternative Dispute Resolution (ADR). She has received the Vanderford Engagement Award, Vanderford Distinguished Teaching Award and the prestigious Neely Award for Teaching Excellence in 2013 at UCO.

PART III

Questioning Upside Down and Backwards: Thinking Differently about Learning

At its heart, learning is letting go of preconceptions or momentary placements to probe new territory. This section offers examples of how thinking through new models, questions, or moments can help create new vision and new questions on your learning journey.

15

CHAPTER FIFTEEN

Daniel Vincent, Ph.D.

Reframing the "Aha!" Moment

We all have heard the stories; we may have even experienced it ourselves. Someone, somewhere, is working on a problem, when, all of a sudden, a light bulb goes on and the "Aha!" moment occurs. It is like a divine revelation— an inspired moment when one gets it, like a switch being tuned on. In fact, the light bulb "thought bubble" is a virtual universal symbol of someone finding an answer or coming up with an idea. It is seductive in its appeal; to know that answers might suddenly get switched on in the brain; the light overtaking the darkness of confusion. To be honest, as a student/learner I have often longed for these "Aha!" moments. I had heard and believed in the "knowledge is power" mantra, and I wanted knowledge so I could be empowered.

However, what I have come to believe as a teacher is, I am doing my students a disservice if I frame my teaching with the expectation that my students experience these "Aha!" moments, where knowledge descends like a dove from the heavens. I have also learned that I, myself, don't crave the moments of insight as much as I now crave something entirely different. For me, I have reframed my "Aha!" moment.

I had my first formal teaching job in 1999 as a 21-year-old fresh out of college; as a science education major, I was confident about the science I knew. I also had strong opinions about what good teaching was. I had lots of "Aha!" moments in college related to my understanding of science, so I assumed that I could relay these same moments to students. In fact, my understanding of science as a discipline was so naïve that I thought science was simply a body of knowledge (some use the phrase "Nature of Science," or just simply NOS, to label what science is and how science works). The more science content a person knew, the better scientist that person was. As such, the role of a science teacher was to develop creative ways to pass on this 'body' of knowledge to their students. I had found success in knowing the science ideas, so, naturally I wanted to pass that feeling of success on to my students.

As I taught through my first year in the profession, I had a sinking feeling that something wasn't quite right with how I taught my students. I also felt that I might be missing something in my understanding of science as a discipline. My students hadn't experienced as many "Aha!" moments as I had hoped, and although many seemed to enjoy my class, it didn't feel as though students were as excited about science as I was. If one were to walk by my class, they would probably see hands-on science occurring, but deep down, I was insecure about what I was doing.

Fast forward a few years through more insecure teaching (even though I tried to come across as confident and in control). I enjoyed teaching, and I suppose some of my students enjoyed learning in my class. I still, however, clung to the idea that science was, at its foundation, a body of knowledge, and as such, my job as a teacher was to convey this knowledge to students. My understanding of good science teaching was grounded in my understanding of the Nature of Science. It wasn't until I worked through graduate school that I encountered an idea that deeply shook my understanding of what science was and how it worked. Although I don't recall the exact moment or experience or text I encountered, I do recall lying in bed, unable to sleep; it was unnerving and disorienting to me. I had assumed that science was a body of knowledge, but somewhere I had completely missed that science is *also* a process humans use to make sense of the world around them. It is a process in which people seek out explanations for questions; the seeking is just as much the science (or more so) as the knowing.

> *I had completely missed that science is also a process humans use to make sense of the world around them. It is a process in which people seek out explanations for questions; the seeking is just as much the science (or more so) as the knowing.*

Intellectually, I began to recognize that I had deep misunderstanding about how science worked, and more fundamentally, what science was. I had a major "Aha!" moment, but it wasn't the type I had longed for or was familiar with. I wasn't adding to what I already knew, but instead, my fundamental ideas about science were being challenged; my "Aha!" moment was the exact opposite. I realized I *did not* understand something that I had long assumed I knew. It troubled me deeply.

Looking back, I can see why it was troubling; the foundations of what I thought I knew were crumbling. My worldview was being challenged. However, knowing what I know now, I can honestly say this event was likely *the* event in my life that began to transform my understanding of teaching and learning. My realized ignorance was the impetus for my change, and according to some, it is a vital step in the learning process. There are even different labels given to this intellectual discomfort (maybe even distress!): "disequilibrium," or "cognitive conflict," or "cognitive dissonance." For me, this moment of confusion was the starting point of my own transformative moment, but it wasn't because someone had intentionally provided answers. It was because I was given the chance to consider what I did not know.

Personally, I feel most transformative learning moments hinge on the "Aha!" moments of realized ignorance. As learners, we are driven by curiosity, and as I realized my own ignorance, I was driven to search for understanding. This search subsequently led me to rebuild my ideas on what science was and how it worked. The rebuilding still continues to this day.

Because of this experience as a learner, I began to reconsider my role as the teacher in a classroom. When I entered the teaching profession, my view of teaching was driven by content and by answers. Because I knew more content and was the expert in the room, I felt it was my responsibility to impart my own understanding to my students. It was a very traditional view of learning, teaching, and of education. I recognize the importance of knowledge, of content, and of facts within the discipline domains; I am not trying to downplay the vital role these play in thinking and decision-making. However, what if we changed our mindset as teachers to

> *However, what if we changed our mindset as teachers to embrace not telling students answers? What if we searched for "Aha!" moments that lead to realized ignorance in our students?*

embrace not telling students answers? What if we searched for "Aha!" moments that lead to realized ignorance in our students? Not that we are purposely trying to make our students feel inferior, but what if we spent our own preparation time working on the questions of our own discipline that would cause students to rethink what they know?

Personally, as I have tried to reframe my own teaching—to move students towards the different "Aha!" moments—I have found both successes and challenges. It was not easy letting go of all the content I felt was important for my students to know. However, seeing and hearing the students get curious about ideas, and work with peers to make sense of it, became educationally satisfying to me. For me, I now find more enjoyment in *uncovering* content, rather than *covering* it—of trying to look deeper into the things I think I understand, instead of explaining things like I do understand them. Each semester, in my own college classroom, there is typically one big "Aha!" moment, in which I realize with my students that I am woefully ignorant on a topic. And I confess my ignorance to my students. Some of my students also came to enjoy the process of having "Aha!" moments in class. As a teacher, I can honestly say that some students never feel comfortable getting pressed this way, and I understand their reluctance. However, I feel this realized ignorance makes for better learners—students who are more skeptical about what they know for certain are more readily able to listen to ideas.

Although I don't have all the answers for how to make this work in a classroom with students, I have found some things that work for me in my setting. As I seek to improve my own understanding of teaching and learning, this list evolves; I am under no illusion that the ideas here are future proof—that they will still be my thoughts five, or ten years from now.[1] Despite that, I'll include some suggestions on how I seek to reframe the "Aha!" moment in my own teaching:[2]

- Search for events, articles, or phenomenon that cause students to question what they know (or what they think they know). Sometimes, and for good reason, students find this upsetting. They cannot understand why they don't understand, or they resist thinking about something they already 'know.'

- Start your semester by sharing the 'big questions' of the course, including the ones you don't know the answer to. Most classrooms are filled with answers, but do students really understand the questions? You could even do this throughout the semester at the beginning or ending of individual classes.

- Don't let students use 'academic vocabulary' when answering questions. In science, for example, most of the vocabulary is conceptual. Personally, I have realized more of my own ignorance when I cannot use an academic term; it forces me to explain, conceptually, my understanding (or lack thereof).

- Encourage, or even force, students to ask questions about the content they encounter.

- Before providing students with disciplinary explanations (in the form of readings, lectures, videos), pose the questions to them and see what they think. I have found that when students attempt to explain an idea before reading about it, students become much more engaged in trying to understand readings or lectures.

- Look for ways to structure your class so discussions are imbedded purposefully and frequently; small group discussions can be wonderful for sharing ideas in low-stress environments.[3]

- Set aside 5 minutes of class where only questions can be asked—no answers and no opinions given—only questions. Also, teach students to ask questions.[4]

- Realize there will be challenges. Curiosity is easy; learning is hard. From my experience, getting students to a place of curiosity is a much easier task compared to helping them satisfy that curiosity through thinking. Most students (or even humans in general) prefer to have answers given to them and some view anything else as 'inefficient' learning. I am guilty of this myself. Sometimes my own curiosity stops at the front door of learning; I don't do the hard work of trying to make sense of things that confuse me.

- Finally, I would challenge any teacher to proclaim their own "Aha!" moments when students are around—in class, in passing, or while talking one-on-one. Get excited about your own ignorance and be willing to share in that excitement.

In closing, I will share a quote that has been attributed to several different people (and phrased several different ways), none of which I can definitely say was first. I share the quote with my students almost every semester, and it has become a driving force in searching for my own reframed "Aha!" moments.

"The greatest barrier to learning is not ignorance; it is the illusion of understanding."

DANIEL VINCENT

Dr. Daniel Vincent is currently a professor of education at the University of Central Oklahoma, specializing in science teaching in K-12 schools. He has almost 20 years of teaching experience, half of those in public schools and half at the university level. Dr. Vincent has written multiple articles related to science teaching/learning, given numerous presentations at the state and national level, and has been recognized for his teaching by earning several awards. Dr. Vincent is married and has two kids; he and his family enjoy traveling around locally in Oklahoma, as well as experiencing cultures far from his home state. In 2010, Vincent received the Neely Excellence in Teaching award.

16

CHAPTER SIXTEEN

David Bass, Ph.D.

How Reading a Book Prevented the Extinction of a Dinosaur

It seems that I was destined to become a professor and pursue a life in academia. It is in my heritage. My father, a lifelong educator, was a high school biology teacher and his mother, my grandmother, taught first grade children for over 40 years. When I was not in school or pursuing athletic activities, I spent much of my childhood outdoors wandering through forests, wading in streams, and collecting shells washed up on the beach. Then I would insist upon telling anyone who would listen what I had learned about the specimens I collected or observations I made while exploring the outdoors, just like a teacher might do. I was fascinated by anything having to do with the sciences and some of my friends even began referring to me as the "professor." It was during this adolescent period that I developed a genuine interest in natural history, and in particular, the small invertebrates that dominate the animal life on Earth today.

During my undergraduate and graduate years as a student, I was fortunate to take a number of courses from professors who were not only highly respected in their discipline but were also outstanding at teaching. Those professors showed me the importance of being a very good teacher. I was inspired by them and emulated their practices in my own endeavors.

I have always worked hard and taken pride in my ability to teach. I prepared for every class period creating detailed notes for that particular group of students. Special attention was paid to the words used to describe concepts and how these ideas were presented. I carefully considered examples and case studies that I believed the students would find relative and easily understand. An hour prior to each lecture was set aside to read through these notes and focus my mind on the upcoming subject matter, so I would be well prepared and on top of my game when I walked into the classroom. The end-of-semester course evaluations prepared by my students always resulted in superior ratings and this underscored my belief that I was doing an excellent job in the classroom. Needless to say, I felt confident in this area of my career.

During my first 20 years as a faculty member, I had a fairly rigid attitude regarding my approach toward student learning. I knew how I learned best and assumed that if a method worked for me, it should work for everyone else. When I look back on those past years, I realize how wrong I was, and frankly, I am a bit embarrassed by that self-centered attitude. Basically, I thought there was only one "best" way to present a concept to everyone. If a student did not understand the concept as presented, I thought they were being lazy and did not apply themselves enough to grasp the concept. I would suggest to students who were doing poorly in my classes that possibly they might understand the material better if they would improve their study habits or possibly took the course from another instructor. Looking back now, I am uncertain if I really believed that was true.

One of the reasons I enjoy being a professor at the University of Central Oklahoma is because this institution places its highest commitment to educating students. While this seems like a no-brainer (I mean, this is a university), they are constantly providing opportunities to educate faculty on how to improve their teaching. In a world where not all educational institutions have shown this degree of commitment, it is a pleasure to work in an environment where teaching excellence is supported so strongly.

> *Now I often stop during the presentation to ask questions that lead to the students using what they know to discover the answers for themselves.*

A week prior to the beginning of the fall 2005 semester, I attended a 50-minute seminar, presented in UCO's Teaching Colloquium, *What the Best College Teachers Do*. It centered around the newly published book bearing the same title by Dr. Ken Bain.[1] Two fellow faculty members who had recently read the book were excited to present their thoughts and share what they learned.

At the end of the seminar, an announcement was made that a book club would be formed and everyone who participated would receive a free copy of Bain's book. I found the seminar discussion intriguing and am a sucker for free stuff, so of course, I signed up. I also thought it would be both enlightening and enjoyable to discuss this topic of teaching excellence with colleagues from different academic disciplines across campus.

The proposed schedule for the book club was to meet for an hour every other week over lunch during the fall semester, completing the book before the Thanksgiving break. Our assignment was to read a couple of chapters each week on our own time and be prepared to discuss them at our bi-weekly gatherings.

Much to my surprise, I became completely immersed in this book. This was partly because I have always thought we could not be taught how to teach, and I still believe that to some degree. Before reading Bain's book, I mistakenly assumed his book would be a recipe, listing ways to improve learning in the classroom (thus, another "how to teach" book). Instead, this book challenged my beliefs, causing me to look inward and conduct a self-examination of my approach to teaching.

I was hooked from the beginning. In Chapter 1 of *What the Best College Teachers Do*, Dr. Bain explained this book was not simply his thoughts on what makes a person an excellent teacher. Instead, it is the result of research into what recognized outstanding teachers do and think and see if the lessons learned by the investigators could improve the teaching by others. As a scientist, I appreciated this research-based approach.

When we gathered to discuss the book, the conversations were interesting and often very thought-provoking, and they continued to challenge me to alter my ideas on how to teach effectively to all of my students. The meetings were so fascinating it was difficult for us to wrap up our discussions by the end of our lunch hours. It became apparent this book club would require more than a few weeks to read and fully discuss the topics presented by Bain, so members of the group decided to continue our lunch meetings past the Thanksgiving break and into the spring semester.

It became evident during the next several weeks how much reading and discussing this book impacted my teaching. My enthusiasm did not go unnoticed and when the original leader could no longer attend our group meetings, I was asked to lead the book club activities. I quickly discovered that I really enjoyed this new role and found parallels that showed me, just as with teaching, the person leading the activities must always be well prepared. I began to think even more deeply about approaches to teaching and what I was reading as I prepared for each week's discussion.

Near the end of the spring semester, shortly after the discussions were completed and the book club had disbanded, the UCO Director of Faculty Enhancement contacted me. He described a 3-day training workshop being offered by Dr. Bain during June at Montclair State University in New Jersey. Funding to send a UCO faculty member to the workshop and bring back a similar program to UCO had been arranged. I felt honored and excited when I was told I had been selected for this opportunity, and immediately placed the workshop dates on my calendar!

About 80 faculty members from across the United States and

Canada attended the workshop at Montclair State University. We spent three days working in small groups, addressing questions posed by Dr. Bain and discussing ideas presented in his book. We also listened to some of the people of whom he wrote and followed up their thoughts with exercises related to their presentations. All of these people were outstanding teachers and it was equally intriguing and stimulating to watch them practice their craft.

One of the most memorable exercises we conducted at the workshop required each of us to select a course we regularly teach and write a brief description of that course. Then we were to imagine this was the "first class day" and we had two minutes to give an oral presentation introducing the course to the students and stimulate them using that description. My personal highlight of this entire workshop was when Dr. Bain noted my presentation was the best example of what should excite a student to learn at a high level, and that is the goal everyone should be striving to obtain! This certainly boosted my confidence that I was on the right track to improve my teaching skills.

It was also encouraging during the workshop to meet other professors from around the nation who were determined to improve their teaching skills. Some of us would venture across the Hudson River and into New York City to eat dinner at the end of each day. As might be suspected among a group of academics, we continued discussing university teaching issues during those meals. It was a wonderful experience to discuss these topics and hear each other's thoughts with so many highly respected colleagues in different disciplines from a diversity of colleges and universities.

Upon returning from Dr. Bain's workshop, I agreed to organize a 3-day seminar for faculty, again titled *What the Best College Teachers Do*. It was to be based on what I had learned while attending Dr. Bain's workshop. I was excited to share the knowledge I had gained with my faculty colleagues, but nervous about whether a seminar conducted by me could actually help them to improve their abilities to effectively teach. In some respects, I felt like the proverbial "fish out of water." Again, I had to think deeply and be prepared more than ever before to lead people through discussions aimed to improve teaching effectiveness.

The seminar took place only a few weeks after I returned, just prior to the beginning of the 2006 fall semester. Before the seminar began, each participant was given a signed copy of Dr. Bain's book and instructed to be prepared to discuss its contents during the three-day event. Time seemed to fly by during each day of the seminar and all appeared to go well. Thoughtful discussions ensued with every topic and each participant told me they felt as if they would be a better teacher from the experience. The provost declared that UCO was a better academic institution as a result of this seminar for faculty. Since then, I have had several opportunities to present variations of this workshop.

So, what have I learned over the years? I have come to realize I am a "dinosaur" that had a dated approach to teaching. My years as an undergraduate and graduate student were during a time when faculty spent almost every class period lecturing while students furiously took notes to use as they prepared for exams. Our overall course grades were determined primarily by scores on our lecture exams, laboratory practicals, and an occasional term paper. This is how almost every undergraduate and graduate course I took in college was conducted. As a student, I learned that if I worked hard enough, then I would probably do well in the course.

> *I have come to understand different students may learn in different ways and often there are several ways that are effective when it comes to how people learn.*

Because this was the format for which I was most familiar, and I had been successful as a student, this was how I approached teaching, and I was comfortable with that for many years.

Reading *What the Best College Teachers Do*, led to a transformation in my approach to teaching and how I conducted my classes. Questions posed by Dr. Bain caused me to think deeply and reflect about why and how topics are covered in the classroom. Often this reflection led me to make changes, not necessarily in the material covered, but how it was presented. I have come to understand different students may learn in different ways and often there are several ways that are effective when it comes to how people learn.

Do I still use the lecture format in my classes? Yes, because all of the seven courses I teach are information rich and providing concise explanations to learners is absolutely necessary for a basic understanding of the subject matter. Many of these changes I implemented seem small, but they do appear to improve student learning. For example, in the past I simply provided students with all the information they needed to understand a concept during a lecture. Now I often stop during the presentation to ask questions that lead to the students using what they know to discover the answers for themselves. This subtle, but important shift, engages the students and allows them to think more deeply about the subject, so they learn from that experience. I had to adjust my approach and tolerate the period of silence that sometimes followed a question while students pondered the possible explanations.

Indeed, old "dinosaurs" like me can change. We can evolve and be transformed, so we do not go extinct as educators. Sometimes all it takes is to look inward and think deeply about what we are doing and why we are doing it to reach our full potential as educators.

DAVID BASS

Dr. David Bass is a Professor of Biology & Curator of Invertebrates at the University of Central Oklahoma where he teaches courses in the fields of invertebrate zoology and ecology. He received a Ph.D. (Zoology) from Texas A&M University and M.S. (Biology) and B.S. (Science Education) degrees from Lamar University. Dr. Bass also served as a Fulbright Professor and Visiting Research Fellow at the University of the West Indies during 1995–1996. His research activities focus on the ecology and biogeography of invertebrates in North America and the Caribbean region. Dr. Bass is a member of several professional societies, including serving as executive director for the Oklahoma Academy of Science and is a past president of the National Association of the Academies of Science. He was named a fellow by the American Association for the Advancement of Science in 2009 for his dedication to science education, original research, and professional service. In 2011, Bass received the Neely Excellence in Teaching award.

17

CHAPTER SEVENTEEN

Wayne Stein, Ph.D.

The Transformational Dreams of a Warrior of Luminosity

"Meditation on inevitable death should be performed daily. Every day when one's body and mind are at peace, one should meditate upon being ripped apart by arrows, rifles, spears and swords, being carried away by surging waves, being thrown into the midst of a great fire, being struck by lightning, being shaken to death by a great earthquake, falling from thousand-foot cliffs, dying of disease or committing seppuku at the death of one's master. Every day without fail one should consider himself as dead."

Hagakure: The Book of the Samurai – Yamamoto Tsunetomo

A Dream of Luminance

To live is to die, for one day everyone dies. Such becomes the retold tale of every human in every culture in every epoch. However, when practicing the spirit of the warrior, the emphasis remains toward the opposite state where to die is to live within a tale of mortality. The act of dying daily becomes our transformational paths towards positive potentials. However, since our daily struggles block our forward momentum, we don't always perceive the karmic points that can guide us towards the brightness.

As a warrior of transformation, I grew up loving samurai, *wuxia pian* (Chinese sword films), and kung fu films. Even the old television show called *Kung Fu* (1972–1975) about a half-Chinese and half-American filled me with dreams of fulfillment, entertainment, and endangerment. I was a happy Hapa, half-Asian and half-American, moving around the frontier as our family lived in various places. Besides the wandering Shaolin monk character, Hollywood also created other parallel tales which I thought were merely science fiction forms of Hapa, people constructed of opposing origins. I enjoyed the reruns of *Star Trek* where Spock, the half-Vulcan and half-human, spoke to my inner chemistry. Actually, both characters were illusions of Hollywood fantasies, having absolutely nothing to do with me. Those Hollywood dreams were mere low shadow beams projected upon my soul that hungered for true images of my warrior's spirit.

Welcome to these warrior adventures in the land of dead fantasies. I was not born in this Western dream. Instead, I was born in a Korean dream, my homeland. Though my mother dreamt me into existence, my father adopted me and introduced me to the Wild West and took me to his California dream. Before leaving, we lived in the Heartland watching martial arts films and learning karate before it was popular, for my father had trained in the famous Mas Oyama dojo in Japan when we lived there and taught me the Kyokushin Way as a kid. I learned to punch with power as I practiced diligently in the way of the warrior.

Then came Bruce Lee, the ultimate cinematic warrior, who changed my life. Bruce said that a warrior has to train hard and be in the best shape, so I was looking for ways to train better.

I developed another warrior love: running, so I joined the track team in the eighth grade. I thought I was the fastest in the Midwest. However, I was shocked when some seventh graders could easily beat me. I suddenly realized that I would not be able to compete on the varsity team. Then I noticed that no one wanted to run the 440-yard dash. The fastest runners wanted the glory of the 100-yard dash while others seemed to prefer long-distance races, so I saw my opening and made my move. Though I didn't like the 440, I was able to compete regularly on the varsity team. I was happy warrior. I even had days off for track meets. Life was good!

Every race seemed the same race. We would line up, and the gun would go off. We would run as fast as we could into the first turn. However, you have to pace yourself, and this was a crucial strategy, the race inside the race. For about three-quarters into the race, we all seemed to run in a pack, very close together. Finally, the last 100 yards would come into view as we turned the last corner. Then the real final race began as everyone kicked as hard as he could. Every warrior must have thought the same, "This is my race. . . my battle. . . my victory."

Every race ended the same for the entire season as I finished last. However, the last race of the season was different. Though I was not winning, my team was one of the best in the state. So, we were in a regional championship. In my final race of the season, I ran against the fastest runner in the state.

The gun went off. We all ran together at first and, as the final turn came upon us, the real race began. Just like every race of the season, it looked like I was going to be last. I had a dream that I would not be last. So, I pushed and pushed myself, and then at the final moment, a miracle happened as I passed the runner in front of me. For the first, last, and the only time, I was not last. I was in the penultimate place.

Then doom arrived as the coach screamed out my name after the race. I felt depressed and devastated as I was about to be yelled at in front of my peers. Thus, this is how a warrior dies. He gathered the team around me. I wasn't going to cry. I was prepared, standing there emotionless, exhausted, trying to breathe, trying to look strong. The coach didn't look happy as the blood veins in his neck popped out and as he yelled out his announcement: "I would prefer you win. When you defeat yourself, that is the best you can ever do in life. I know that Wayne trains just as hard as anyone on this team. I have seen him throw up from exhaustion after practice. Do your best in life, all of you! If you break your own time, you are a winner in my book. Wayne broke his own time!" Then he started to applaud as the rest of the team joined in the celebration. The team was actually happy for me, not mad at me for losing. I was in shock experiencing a warrior's dream of luminance.

A Dream of Radiance

My father moved us westward to California where he was born. I recall the first day at school when my mother drove me to enroll at the very middle school of Marilyn Monroe. My mother had seen her personally in Korea. This school is where some scenes from the musical *Grease* with John Travolta and Olivia Newton John were shot. After we walked into the administration office, she tried to politely get some help. No one noticed her. I was a bit frustrated and used to this. My mother, being Asian, was often not listened to at stores; this was those pre-Walmart days, when you had to have a real reason to bring back something you bought. So, I puffed out my chest as a warrior, rapped my knuckles on the table, and raised my voice asking for assistance. Then there came a strange silence in this California dream. Everyone froze, made strange faces, and starred at me. Then a lady asked, "Where were you born?" I answered, "Korea." Confused she asked, "And where did you learn to speak English?" I answered, "OK-LA-HO-MA! The land of the red man! Flash! Amazing fact, they all seem to speak English there. I never met anyone that spoke Cherokee. Just English." I thought to myself, these people are crazy. What dream world are they living in?

The lady laughed. She then helped me. I showed her my grades of A from an Arizona school where we had stopped for a few weeks, living in some mobile home reject, before leaving and coming to the California Dream. When I entered the hallway going to my first class, I noticed something. None of the students walking to their classes spoke

English. They mostly spoke Spanish while others spoke Korean or Chinese. Now I understood her questions.

Then we walked outside to another building. The first impression I had was that the school looked, smelled, and felt like a prison with hall monitors who substituted as guards and barbed wires on top of the walls. In my imagination, I could see machine guns in the towers. The school was surrounded by roads on all sides. If there were some sort of flood, and all the roads were filled with murky water, I guarantee the school would look exactly like Alcatraz, which I had visited.

During my physical education class, we were bused daily to a picturesque park in the mountain side since there was no gymnasium. Walking down the bus stairs on the first day, someone kicked me in the back, welcoming me. With that, the California dream started to merge into a nightmare as I hit the ground hard. I stood up like a warrior, smiling with my chest out. Everyone behind me acted like nothing happened. Later, a Chinese friend came up and told me that Carlos, a gang member, had kicked me. I didn't retaliate because fighting friends of his brotherhood would be senseless. This prison was different than normal prisons because we struggled, escaped, and returned daily voluntarily. Attending this school was hard for any warrior. Even if you could fight, you wouldn't fight back like in *The Karate Kid*. Fighting becomes a form of losing, for someone will use yearbook images as mug shots to identify you as the guilty one.

> *I was transformed by this technique of critical creativity. To this day, I require in almost all my classes that my students be creative as they rewrite, revise, and rethink the art of narratives.*

Why would any instructor voluntarily teach at this prison of stress? Though I hated the school, I met some of the kindest teachers in all my years of going to school. Indeed, I was amazed at these teachers, for they earned the respect of the students. Indeed, most were fantastic instructors. My history teacher was a masterful storyteller. He made World War II interesting for all. When he had five minutes or so to spare, he just made up funny stories, where we became characters. Thus, he made us listen, laugh, and learn.

I now use such storytelling techniques in my own classes because of him. I was transformed by this technique of critical creativity. To this day, I require in almost all my classes that my students be creative as they rewrite, revise, and rethink the art of narratives. In my English composition class, I even created a cyberpunk gaming virtual reality where students write science fiction narratives. Being creative remains a form of transformational learning.

With predicable dread, I went to prison daily even though I had such amazing teachers. Then one day, the teacher in physical education announced: "Track Meet." He told everyone to practice, and we did. As we practiced, I intentionally lost every time. After all, that is what I did best, but this time I knew something they didn't. They thought I was not very athletic. Many of them were out of shape. Some even smoked cigarettes. Then the day of the meet came. I entered three events: the 440 (one lap), the 880 (two laps), and the long jump. As we lined up for the 440, I noticed Carlos to my right. The race began and I intentionally ran last. As we entered the final turn, they started to kick. I watched them. This seemed like déjà vu. Then I kicked, and I easily passed everyone, including Carlos, winning by about 15 yards. I also won the 880 and the long jump. No contest. Something happened after that day. I won something else: respect. Not everyone noticed me, but Carlos and others no longer messed with me. They gave me room. At times, they even yelled out my name as a sign of respect. I still have those ribbons as a memento of a warrior's dream of radiance.

A Dream of Imminence

My next dream year, I went to Fairfax High School. Paramount Studios was on the way home from Fairfax. On Fridays, I often watched them film *Happy Days* for free. The most famous star was Henry Winkler who portrayed Fonzie. One evening, he came out and shook hands, and I was last. As I shook his famous hand, nervously, I said, "Fonzie can you give me your autograph?" Oh, he did not look happy as he said, "First of all, my name is not Fonzie! Secondly, I don't give autographs because it isn't fair to all those whom I already shook hands with."

I heard laughter from my friends as the superstar walked away. My laughing Asian and Hispanic friends represented the new Los Angeles while on stage was the old Hollywood fantasy of white America. Strange that the old white majority no longer lived in the multicultural Los Angeles. Stars had to drive from the upper-class hills or mountains down to places like Paramount Studios, still located within the city. My friends always made fun of me from this incident. At the time, the fantasy factory of La La Land, Hollywood, seemed out of place and lacked any multicultural vision that meant things to the real people of Los Angeles.

Los Angeles did have some of the most amazing bookstores I have even seen, so I started to read multicultural literature: Latin American, African American, and Asian literature.

Those books were transformational to me. Gabriel Garcia Marquez became my favorite writer. The world literature book I had as a university student was Eurocentric in nature, not global. Today, I proudly teach Garcia Marquez and magical realism in my World Literature 2 course. So, I am currently invoking a revolution of intellectual revenge by teaching what had never been taught to me.

Concerning Asians in cinema, not much has changed with Hollywood. Asian films or television shows are still rare in Hollyweird. Bruce Lee, an Asian American warrior, died some 40 years ago. There has never been another male Asian American superstar. Jackie Chan, born in Hong Kong, is not American.

When are the Asians going to start protesting? I am happy to teach Asian American literature and Asian cinema, providing honest and unique perspectives. Not much has changed in the art of White Washing Asian culture. Some eighty years ago, Luise Rainer won an academy award for playing the Chinese woman, O-Lan in *The Good Earth* (1937), while Linda Hunt won Best Supporting Actress for playing a Hapa male, Billy Kwan, in *The Year of Living Dangerously* (1982).

My happy days as a Hapa in Los Angeles seemed to be a cultural awakening of the warrior's dream of imminence.

A Dream of Translucence

Flash forward to another dream, some ten or more years later. This is an important tip for a future teacher: have passion and enthusiasm. I was about to graduate with a degree. I loved to read and took literature classes for fun to break up the monotony of so many computer programming courses. However, finding programming so boring and not satisfying, I went with my warrior's heart and switched to my real passion by becoming an English major. I wasn't sure what do to with an English degree.

I graduate from college, and I return to Korea, my homeland. Not having returned since I left as a child, I teach all three grades at an elite college prep high school. In the first class, the tenth grade, I am worshiped. They are exuberant, laugh at my bad jokes, and happy to have me as their teacher. In the eleventh-grade classes, they are less joyful of my existence. Then someone asks if I speak Korean. I reply no. Someone else under his breath calls me stupid in Korean. I walk up to him, smile, and look him in the eyes and proclaim, "I am not stupid." He turns fifty shades of red as everyone laughs. In the last class of seniors, on the board, these words are written: "ET (English teacher) go home!" I laugh as I erase the words and think as a warrior, "I am home. I am finally home." From these students, I learned a lot about who I was to become. Though I wasn't the best teacher, I found my home. I knew that I only wanted to do one thing in life: teach.

I have become the teachers I have learned from by mirroring their lessons and by sharing their pedagogical creativity with my students. Therefore, death dies as life is reborn while experiencing a shared dream luminating each other.

I returned to Oklahoma where I started. Death is not the final moment of living. Why? Because we return and are reborn as one moment is transformed into another moment of positive awakening of the interconnectivity of existence!

I have become the teachers I have learned from by mirroring their lessons and by sharing their pedagogical creativity with my students. Therefore, death dies as life is reborn while experiencing a shared dream luminating each other. We are all action stars within our karmic cinematic struggles.

The warrior within knows that death remains the only way of living with the gradual dissolutions of the ego, the awakening of the third eye with its dreams of luminance, the shedding of the skin, the floating within the dreams of radiance, the merging into the darkness within the dreams of imminence, into the everythingness towards the community of eternal souls or suns, the entering into a secret phantom home of clarity not found in the battles of life, the smiling at the warrior of transformation, the projecting of lucid dreams within a dream of translucence.[1]

WAYNE STEIN

Dr. Wayne Stein, Doc Nirvana the warrior of learning, teaches courses on Asian Cinema of Horror, Films of Akira Kurosawa, Kung Fu Cinema, and Bruce Lee Cinema. Being the advisor to the university Budo Society, the Way of the Warrior, he voluntarily teaches Japanese martial arts to students. He co-edited a book on the filmmaker Yasujiro Ozu. Becoming a vegetarian recently, he ended years of suffering from stomach pain. He is creating his own martial arts style emphasizing *neidan*, the breathing techniques of Chinese alchemy as its foundation. He has incorporated lucid dream transformational theory as a way of learning levels of knowledge in his History of Rhetoric and Jackie Chan Cinema courses. Critical creative thinking assignments of storytelling are in almost all of his classes to make students understand the power of the imagination as they ponder critically. In 2005, Stein received the Neely Excellence in Teaching award.

18

CHAPTER EIGHTEEN

Joselina Cheng, Ph.D.

A Strategic Nautilus Model and Innovative Toolbox

"Problems cannot be solved with the same mindset that created them."

–Albert Einstein

The proliferation of new technologies has changed the way people live, teach, learn, and work. Although the future of work is unclear, experts envision a new machine age where technologies such as Internet of Things (iOT), machine learning, artificial intelligence (AI), and analytics will be embedded around, on, and in us. Thus, this emerging Human-Technology frontier is where technologies will influence our student experiential learning experiences, transformative education, and the quality of work life. Without question, the U.S. workforce will need a new set of skills and competencies in order to succeed in the future work environments on this frontier. According to research, work environments at the Human-Technology Frontier include, but are not limited to, the characteristics of: life-long learning, interdisciplinary collaboration, data focus, computational thinking, problem-based solution, agility, disruption, and innovation.

Indeed, higher education bears the responsibility to better prepare today's digital learners for the future workforce. However, with technologies (e.g., iOT, AI) that continue to emerge and new jobs yet to be created, how do educators teach something that has not yet existed? While there are no quick solutions to answer the above questions, one thematic finding derived from literature is that *our students must become agile learners and adaptable citizens in order to compete and succeed in the global economies.* This finding aligns with my teaching philosophy and practices to: (1) teach our students with real-world applications, (2) equip them with foundational/transferable skills, and (3) inspire them to be a life-long learner by learning how to learn. To support my teaching philosophy, sections below first present a reflection of my personal learning journey. Then followed with discussions of how I incorporated my personal experiences, industry background, and teaching principles of *UCO's Educational Philosophy* to build upon UCO's transformative-learning (TL) tenants. By leveraging emerging human-technology to create innovative teaching and learning toolbox, I extended learning spaces beyond the traditional brick-and-mortar classrooms. Evidence-based practices also allowed me to better prepare today's digital learners for the future workforce by helping students acquire the 21st century skills with experiential learning and transformative education.

A Reflective Journey

A paradigm shift occurred when I switched from the IT industry to academia after working as a project director for 20 years, managing software design and development for Fortune 500 Companies. I noticed a gap that existed in the skills sets between what employers are looking for and what newly graduated students possessed. Thus, I started my teaching career in higher education with a passion to better prepare students by leveraging technologies so that they can compete in highly global economies. I soon realized that simply having technical competency was insufficient to help students succeed. To become a better teacher, I needed to become a life-long learner. Sections below describe three salient aspects of my personal learning journey when searching for transformative educational models, teaching strategies, and innovative learning tools to help students succeed.

Salient Aspect # 1 of My Personal Learning Journey: Andragogy (Adult Learning)

Searching for best practices led me to the theoretical framework of Knowles' adult learning theory (andragogy). According to Knowles, relevancy is a key ingredient for engaging adult learners in active learning and solving real-life problems. To experience adult learning first-hand, I looked into many doctoral programs to gain the proper perspectives and deepen insights on what relevant, real-life challenges that adult learners faced. One immediate question surfaced, *"How do adult students with full-time jobs attend school?"* While an online degree seemed like the solution, I went for a hybrid program, which required a mixture of face-to-face residence and web-based courses.

For my dissertation, I focused on innovative leadership and e-learning. I interviewed many universities, administrators, and faculty members to identify institutional and instructional deterrent that contributed to a high online course attrition rate and low-quality online education. I also volunteered to serve on the Task Force and Planning committee when UCO began to recognize that adult learners preferred to take online courses due to their flexibility and accommodating features (i.e. adapting a course to accommodate an 8-to-5 working schedule). UCO went from zero to over 400 online and hybrid courses for Spring 2019. In spring 2019, UCO offered a total of 380 online sections consisting of 168 individual courses. For hybrid courses, we are offering 60 online sections consisting of 41 individual courses.

Salient Aspect # 2 of My Personal Learning Journey: Motivational Model

I was exposed to the nautilus model during my residency. Our doctoral cohort was sub-divided into five teams. One assignment was to share something with the most growth potential. Many teams quickly went into the MBA mode and came up with SWOT analysis, product presentation, sales projections, etc. I suggested to my team not to be limited to a product nor a service but something totally different and revolutionary. My team members took a chance on me and we scored the highest because the doctoral faculty thought what we presented was something totally different and revolutionary.

> *I realized that the secret ("aha!" moment) was to reach Maslow's higher/hierarchical order of intrinsic motivation. That is, to achieve our potential, reach self-actualization, and experience fulfillment.*

Our team was the only group that made the connection between the exercise and the Nautilus model with our personal and professional growth. When a nautilus matures, it creates new layers within its existing shell and moves its growing body into the larger space. As a doctoral learner, I was stretched managing school, full-time job, and life events (more in Salient Aspect section below). Yet, I also experienced tremendous growth during my three-year doctoral journey. I realized that the secret ("aha!" moment) was to reach Maslow's higher/hierarchical order of intrinsic motivation. That is, to achieve our potential, reach self-actualization, and experience fulfillment. Thus, after I obtained my Ph.D., I continued to seek learning opportunities to grow personally and professionally through venues of professional development, research, publication, and grantsmanship.

Salient Aspect # 3 of My Personal Learning Journey: Government-University-Industry Model

As stated above, the concept of continuous upgrades with innovative technologies was a common practice, however, it was more difficult to apply in academia with fewer resources. Any changes in organizational culture or policies also took longer for any administration or institution. To overcome the constraints of resources, time, and tools to support teaching, I tapped into my 20 years of IT experience and three years of doctoral studies to think outside the box to support teaching. With this thinking, I began with an internal grant funded with a budget of $500 to now submitting NSF grants with a budget of approximately $1 million. Over a five-year period, I secured R&D funding over millions of dollars. Funding agencies included the Oklahoma State Regents for Higher Education, Experimental Program to Stimulate Competitive Research (EPSCoR), a private foundation, and the National Science Foundation.

In retrospect, what I accomplished was not humanly possible as I lost my husband and my parents to cancer during these same five-year periods. *My faith in God and my belief in making differences in my students' lives sustained me with persistence.* This additional funding allowed me to expand institutional resources, leverage technological infrastructures, and collaborate with external partners. Synergized partnerships included Apple, FBI, Francis Tuttle Innovation Center, IBM, Oklahoma Bureau of Investigation, and Washington Global Health Alliance (funded by Gates' Foundation). Funding which came from these internal and external grants allowed me to study best practices and experiment with innovative teaching and learning tools for adding to or upgrading my toolbox. Additional resources also enabled me to implement the Government-University-Industry (GUI) model with real-world applications and strategic interventions. Students were provided with career-exploration venues, knowledge acquisition, and skill development through job shadowing, mentoring, internships, and research fellowship partnerships. Sections below present discussions of how I implemented the R&D of innovative teaching and learning tools to benefit my students and better prepare them for the highly competitive workforce.

Integrating Personal Experience with Transformative Teaching & Learning

The quest for transformative models to fill the gap led me to

UCO. As stated previously, my passion is to better prepare today's digital learners with 21st century skills by leveraging real-world experiences, emerging technologies, and innovative andragogy (Andragogy is based on Knowl's adult learning theory to motivate students with relevant and real-life scenarios), so that our students can become the workforce participants in highly competitive global economies and rapidly changing knowledge-based societies. Sections below present discussions of how to support my teaching philosophy with hybrid courses and innovative teaching tools to engage students in active, collaborative, and experiential learning. Examples of the impacts of having a diverse portfolio of interactive learning modules, cloud-based tutorials, simulated learning environments, and job shadowing on students' learning outcomes will also be presented when students' challenges, diversity, and learning styles are addressed contextually, andragogically, and technologically.

Addressing Challenges in the 21st Century Classroom

Learning in the 21st century is no longer limited to just a physical classroom in a brick-and-mortar university. Today's digital learners, who live and learn in an immersive environment, prefer learning to occur in a virtual space or outside the classroom. Likewise, non-traditional students with full-time jobs also prefer learning and just-in-time skill acquisition without time and location constraints. Many traditional universities start offering online courses to better accommodate today's adult learners. I was the first instructor who designed online courses for my department and my college. All my online courses, which were reviewed by peers, have scores above 95%. Thus far, all my courses have been certified by the Center for eLearning and Connected Environments (CeCE) with quality seals. Over the years, I encountered some of those challenges identified by literature, including interactivity, collaboration, active learning, timely feedback, currency, relevancy, and high standards of quality education. I address these challenges by applying Chickering and Gamson's (C&G) seven principles. See sections below for examples and suggestions

> *Learning in the 21st century is no longer limited to just a physical classroom in a brick-and-mortar university. Today's digital learners, who live and learn in an immersive environment, prefer learning to occur in a virtual space or outside the classroom.*

regarding how I incorporate C&G principles, teaching strategies, and innovative technologies to help students learn.

Set #1: Strategies & Tools for Student-Faculty Interaction

To encourage student-faculty interactions (C&G Principle #1), students are engaged in multi-channel communications with me via text, email, Facetime, phone, Skype, LinkedIn, office visits, or professional meetings. Mobile apps, tablets, and neuro-pedagogical strategies are used to engage students.

Tips: Tellagami is a very user-friendly mobile app which I incorporate into D2L to increase faculty presence in online courses during an orientation in week 1. Students also create test questions for each chapter. A computer with a pre-programmed algorithm selects 10% of those questions for a semester exam.

Set #2: Strategies & Tools for Service & Transformative Learning

To encourage cooperation among students (C&G Principle #2), group study, team projects and service learning are collaborative strategies for learners to construct knowledge while being socially connected to serve local communities and global stakeholders. For my *Business Analysis & Design* course, one team of students contacted a non-profit organization. The service project started with a manual process without any computers and took donations to purchase wreaths to place on the graves of veterans who gave their lives while defending our country. On average, only about 100 wreath donations could be processed each year. When my student completed the design and development of a web-based system for matching funds, over 2000 wreaths were delivered and placed.

Tips: Faculty members can apply for funding to become a Service Learning Scholar. Faculty members may also be considered and be appointed by the Academic Affairs to become a Transformative Learning Scholar. Either venue provides resources for faculty members to design team assignments for helping non-profit organizations and local communities. Team project assignments can be set up in Desire to Learn (D2L), which is the Learning Management System at UCO. Students' projects will be recorded in the Student Transformative Learning Record in addition to the academic record.

Set #3: Strategies & Tools for Active Learning

To encourage active learning (C&G Principle #3), learning modules are designed with student-centeredness. Flipping strategies are also used to encourage students for taking the lead with classroom discussions while I serve the role of a facilitator. Students are also strongly encouraged to take ownership of their learning process by inputting ideas for any of class project design, the recruitment and selection of team members, assignment due dates, creation of test questions, and student portfolios. Students also reflect upon their learning journey with a digital journal.

Tips: I often use Mind Mapping to engage my students in active learning. Students will apply textbook materials by drawing the conceptual diagrams on the classroom white board. Research shows that Mind Mapping can help students organize their thought process and recall information during testing.

Set #4: Strategies & Tools for Timely Feedback

To give timely feedback (C&G Principle #4), online exams are set up to post grades and feedback automatically and immediately upon submission. Students can review their grades and feedback within 24–48 hours for any paper-based exams or assignments. Students are provided with tutoring to gain a deeper understanding and mastery of skills. Students can resubmit assignments to improve their grades.

Set #5: Strategies & Tools for Job Shadowing & Mentoring

To bring students with experiential learning experiences, *Avaya* simulation technology is used to immerse students in a simulated environment. Students are to role play as a network administrator who fixes IT Security problems (Figure 2). Job-shadowing and role-playing activities can better equip today's learners with 21st century skills so that they can participate fully in an increasingly competitive global economy. The mobile app *Socrative* is used by students to perform peer evaluations while each team presents their group project.

Tips: To help students stay current with emerging trends, IT projects, and time management (C&G Principle #5 time on task), students are engaged in research and professional organizations.

Industry speakers and leaders are often invited to share insights with students on careers, entrepreneurship, internships, IT security, or white-collar crimes. Professionals representing Paycom, the Oklahoma Center for the Advancement of Science and Technology (OCAST) and the FBI are frequent speakers in my classrooms. Students are also engaged in transformative learning activities including the co-authorship of any research papers, co-development of posters for Oklahoma Research Day, and co-presentations with me at national and international conferences.

Set #6: Strategies & Tools for Higher Standards

To communicate high expectations (C&G Principle #6) and where with rapid obsolescence in the IT industry, students are challenged to become better learners and researchers in order to stay current in a knowledge-based society. Assignments are designed to help students acquire and maintain the 21ˢᵗ century skills, knowledge, and abilities. Students are also made aware of the requirements and the grading rubrics, which will be used to assess students' assignments, weekly discussions, and semester-long projects. High standards can better prepare our students to succeed in highly competitive global economies.

Tips: Students are encouraged to generate original content. *Turnitin* software is used for all written assignments and research papers to discourage plagiarism.

Set #7: Strategies & Tools for Accommodating Diverse Learners & Learning Styles

UCO has a distinct advantage: 40% of undergraduate students come from 120 countries. To respect diverse talents and different ways of learning (C&G Principle #7), I strongly encourage domestic students to collaborate with international students for any semester-long team projects. While English may not be the native language for some students, collaboration provides two-way communication, which benefits students by allowing them to gain unique perspectives on problem solving, broadening their global competency, and deepening their cultural understandings. Too often, online courses are plagued with static text-based learning materials which are converted from Power Point slides or lecture notes to PDF files and uploaded to a course management platform such as D2L. As a result, the attrition rate of many online courses can be as high as 75% when students' learning styles are not addressed sufficiently.

Tips: To better address student learning styles and diverse dynamics, I actively engage in research to study global mindset and cultural intelligence. I also sought funding to pilot innovative teaching tools for helping diverse students learn and succeed. One example is that I incorporate cutting-edge technologies such as *Camtasia* to create interactive learning modules and cloud-based tutorials to foster a multi-sensory learning environment. See Set #4 Strategies & Tools for evidence how those multimedia learning tools improve learning outcomes when student learning styles are better addressed.

Set #8: Strategies & Tools for Measuring Success in Helping Students Learn

Helping students succeed is why I became a teacher. Knowing that test scores alone do not define a student, I measure student success with holistic and on-going processes including the (1) R&D and pilot tests to provide evidence that students with exposure and access to innovative tools 24/7 outperformed by one letter grade than those with access to only text-based lectures.

Tips: Additional measures include (2) seeking informal feedback from students throughout the current semester; (3) updating Academic Early Referral System to identify at-risk students so that additional assistance can be rendered via venues including in-person consultation, web-based tutoring, or extended office hours; (4) aligning or exceeding my end-of-semester formative SPIE evaluations with those of my department and college; (5) benchmarking departmental assessments per academic year; (6) serving as mentors for current students for any student-led research, transformative projects, service learning, and internship; and (7) collaborating with former students who are hiring managers via LinkedIn to offer internship or job opportunities. Excerpts below are from former students who are now IT professionals, researchers, and post-doctoral graduates.

"Having Dr. Cheng before this class, I expected the same quality & detail in this class. She is very knowledgeable in the field of computer science. One of the best professors I have ever had."

"Dr. Cheng, taking your class and working with you definitely changed my way of doing things. I have become a better learner, researcher, and I have come to have more confidence in myself. I feel fortunately to be so involved at UCO I attended [sic]. The more involved I am, the more I want to pursue an advanced degree. This is definitely a transformative learning experience."

"Dear Dr. Cheng, I just wanted to thank you. Working with you was a great experience, and it helped propel me to the success I am experiencing now. It acclimated me to certain aspects of the IT profession and has overall been very useful ..."

Embarking on Your Own Journey: Takeaways

I have experienced phenomenal growth in my personal learning journey. I sincerely hope that our students can have a transformative education experience and continue to grow personally and professionally after graduation. I also encourage faculty members to join me in the life-long learning journey by incorporating some of these models, strategies, and tools to build an innovative toolbox to help our diverse learners.

As Jim Collins[1] wrote in his book, *Good to Great*, educators are like "level-5 leaders who set up their successors for even greater success in the next generation" (2001, p. 39). Indeed, true excellence can be achieved by implementing the nautilus model through the transformational process that allows learners to tap into the intellect of each unique person who has the best to offer. When educators understand the purpose that ignites, the vision that motivates, and the value that empowers, students can embark in their own transformative learning journey to acquire the 21st century skills and succeed in the Human-Technology workforce.

JOSELINA CHENG

Dr. Cheng has worked in the information technology industry for 20 years as a project manager, in which she designed, developed, and implemented software for Fortune 500 companies. Dr. Cheng's vision is to transform education by providing today's digital learners with experiential learning through innovative technologies. Dr. Cheng is also a two-time Barnabas Fellow, a distinguished researcher for the ISOM Department, an awardee of 20 fully funded internal and external grants, and a reviewer for the National Science Foundation. She has been recognized for her achievements at UCO, receiving the 2016 Neely Excellence in Teaching Award, 2015 Best Educator Award, 2014 Desire to Learn Impact Award, 2013 Vanderford Initiative Award, and the 2012 Faculty Merit-Credit Award. She is also the recipient of the 21st Century Pedagogy Award. Additional scholarly achievements include 15 peer-reviewed publications. Dr. Cheng is also the designer of Virtual Tutor Learning Systems, published by McGraw-Hill and Prentice Hall. She has presented over 100 topics at regional, national, and international conferences. http://business.uco.edu/faculty-staff-directory/name/joselina-cheng/

19

CHAPTER NINETEEN

J. David Macey, Ph.D.

The Personal Is Pedagogical: Speaking "Out" in the Classroom

M ore than a decade ago, I stood on the lawn of a small liberal arts college, holding a candle and talking with students at the end of a campus vigil. As I was getting ready to leave, a student who had recently caused controversy on campus through a set of seemingly homophobic remarks approached me and thanked me for being present that evening. The student, who would "come out" a few years later, but who at the time scarcely seemed an ally, then said something that I did not expect: "You're the first gay person I've ever met who doesn't work in a bar or the community center." After that, the student hugged me and disappeared into the crowd.

I remember that evening, and I continue to revolve this story in my mind, because they speak to me both as an activist and as an educator. The student and I made a connection, finding common ground in a shared if not yet fully disclosed identity that helped us to bridge our significant differences in age, gender, experience, and ideology. We were able to do so at least in part because I had risked coming out publicly on campus and in the classroom as a gay man, and I had used the critical distance that this identity offers—or imposes on—me to raise questions about personal identity, cultural conventions, and social justice that otherwise might not have been addressed within our largely heterosexual and pervasively heteronormative campus community.

In the early 1970s, Rictor Norton,[1] who taught one of the first college-level courses on gay literature, advised colleagues about the difficult process of engaging in identity-based activism in an academic setting. Even as Norton imagines gay and lesbian faculty members shaking up their classrooms and campuses by "inviting their local Gay Liberation Front to send a panel to class for a candid dialogue" (p. 691), he recommends caution, urging his readers to "always remain as cool and academically righteous as possible" (p. 675) when challenging their students' and colleagues' assumptions and prejudices.

I, too, have felt called upon, time and again, to "keep cool" and to work within the system—indeed, to "work the system"—to achieve acceptance and equality. If my professional training, both as a graduate student and as a teaching assistant, suggested anything about personal identity—especially my personal identity—it was that it had no place in the classroom and that the consequences of coming out on campus would prove, sooner rather than later, to be dire. The personal was emphatically not pedagogical, or at least so my teachers, especially those who were likely gay, lesbian, or bisexual themselves, seemed fervently to believe.

By the time I arrived on the campus of that small liberal arts college, I had come out of the closet in my teaching and in my public persona on campus. I had not done so in a particularly purposeful manner, understanding the pedagogical implications of "outness" with any degree of theoretical sophistication, nor was it my intention, at least on a conscious level, to "queer" my classroom. More than anything else, I had grown frustrated with my colleagues' and students' unspoken assumption that I was probably gay but that I would surely never be so unprofessional—and impolitic—as to acknowledge that fact on campus.

Upon outing myself, I quickly found myself playing a new and often awkward role, both inside and outside of the classroom, as the on-campus spokesperson—or surrogate—for "my people," as a university administrator once uncomfortably referred to the lesbian, gay, bisexual, and transgender (LGBTQ+) community in an effort to acknowledge us without naming us. I felt an obligation to engage colleagues and students in candid, often difficult dialogues about sexuality and the complexly related but distinct category of gender—awkward conversations in which I figured, simultaneously and uncomfortably, both as a participant in and as the topic of discussion. How, I have often wondered, did I become at once the advocate, the interpreter, and the defender of a set of identities, of ways of being in the world that I feel so inadequate, as an older, white, cisgender man from the upper end of the socio-economic spectrum, to represent in their rich and challenging diversity?

I have learned over time that this position, fraught with contradictions, offers both opportunities and challenges to a teacher, especially in a university setting—challenges that can be as real on a West Coast campus as they are in Oklahoma, their subtler manifestations every bit as difficult to address as their more explicit expressions. In continuing to reflect on that night so many years ago, I meditate on what it revealed about the relationship between being "out" as our authentic selves and being "outsiders," sometimes disrupting, often complicating, but ideally enriching our community's lived experience, whatever that community's composition or ideological orientation may be.

Both the student and I, on that long-ago evening, were treading a boundary—a line of demarcation between the familiar and the unknown, between our very different lived experiences and the unexpected common ground that our unplanned interaction exposed. Victor Turner[2] speaks of the special, perilous, but powerful status of "threshold people," who stand within, but also outside of, the professional communities to which they are assigned by avocation or opportunity (p. 95). No longer silenced and cast out, but not yet fully integrated into an institutional culture that we both claim and question, LGBTQ+ faculty members have the opportunity—and, I believe, the obligation—to cultivate an uncomfortable but fruitful middle ground, planting and nurturing the seeds of the world we seek to create for ourselves and for our students. This process is a constitutive element of Transformative Learning because it pushes both teachers and students outside of their comfort zones and challenges them to map hitherto unexplored conceptual territories.

> *LGBTQ+ faculty members have the opportunity—and, I believe, the obligation—to cultivate an uncomfortable but fruitful middle ground, planting and nurturing the seeds of the world we seek to create for ourselves and for our students.*

Narratives about teaching often focus on the process of guiding a diverse group of learners to a common understanding of a set of issues or ideas, moving the classroom community from dissonance to consonance, from multiple positions of (mis)understanding to a new understanding shared by the class as a whole. As Jack Mezirow[3] notes, however, "reaching a consensus is a theoretical goal but not the only function of discourse" within a Transformative Learning environment (p. 170). A complex interplay of consensus and dissent, of making meaning and of acknowledging the experiential limits of our understanding, inflects academic discussions of sexuality and gender; this tension provides an opening for students and their teachers to stake and negotiate new claims about who we are and how we live, both individually and socially. In the process, students and teachers learn to acknowledge an increasingly diverse range of identities and subject positions.

As an instructor, I ask myself what it means to seek shared understanding in a pluralistic learning community composed of individuals with significantly—at times, radically—different experiences, backgrounds, expectations, and goals. We open up a discursive space that is at once exhilarating and cacophonous, empowering but perilous when we decenter authority within the classroom; share our personal experiences of vulnerability, marginalization, and exclusion; and encourage our students to interrogate and contest the competing claims about identity, morality, and public policy that surround issues such as sexuality and gender.

Tensions and anxieties come to surface when students and their teachers engage with these challenging questions in company with others whose lives differ in fundamental ways from their own. The poet, critic, and activist Gloria Anzaldúa[4] examines the effects of "multiple, often opposing messages" in discourse communities composed of individuals with varied, sometimes intersectional and sometimes antithetical identities and values. "The coming together of...self-consistent but habitually incomparable frames of reference," she observes, "causes *un choque*, a cultural collision" (p. 100). Coming out on campus and in the classroom provides an opportunity for instructors and students to harness the transformative potential of this shock to our conceptual systems.

As we move, with our students, beyond the familiar territory policed by academic and social conventions, we enter an uncharted social and intellectual space defined by our differences, both from one another and from the public selves that we have been conditioned to perform. In the process, we become active participants in Transformative Learning. Anzaldúa[5] explores the "transformations [that] occur in this in-between space, [this] unstable, unpredictable, precarious, always-in-transition space lacking clear boundaries" (p. 1) where we encounter, in one another, forms of diversity both expected and unexpected. These transformations are inevitably mutual ones, as was the case that evening on campus so many years ago. The student learned something new about how—and who—one can be in the world, and I learned how firsthand encounters with others' diversity can transform our understanding of ourselves and of our place in the world.

How, where, and to what extent can we as faculty members foster and sustain dialogue within a community of interlocutors whose ways of knowing and strategies for communicating are shaped by experiences of marginalization or empowerment, of alienation or community, to which we have no direct access? I ask this question each time that I enter the classroom at the beginning of a new semester, and each semester I rediscover the importance of owning, to myself and to my students, both my ongoing struggle, only sometimes successful, to find points of intersection between my lived experiences and the texts and traditions that I teach, and the sense of estrangement that I continue to feel from the institutions that have been my professional home for most of my adult life.

"Voyager," Anzaldúa[6] writes, "there are no bridges, one builds them as one walks" (p. v). Students rightly perceive their instructors as academic insiders, as representatives of institutional authority, and as mediators of institutional benefits. As a gay man in a largely heterosexual, pervasively heteronormative, and too often, still explicitly homophobic environment, I feel as though I am as much an outsider as an insider. Decades have passed since I first came out, but I am still building the bridges that I hope, sometimes seemingly against hope, will connect the internal and experiential places where I live most fully as myself with the geographical, disciplinary, and interpersonal geographies that I traverse in my professional life.

This experience of being at once an insider and an outsider, of struggling to integrate my personal identity with my role as the representative of an institution in which I am often ill at ease, helps me to locate a shared ground of experience on which to meet my students, who also grapple with experiences of personal and institutional alienation. Too often, critics and commentators accuse us of sowing the seeds of division in the classroom, or of politicizing—and polarizing—academic discourse when we share and call upon others to recognize and honor our lived experiences of diversity, whether of sexuality, gender, race, ethnicity, class, or ability. Acknowledging and discussing our different, but otherwise unacknowledged, subject positions are essential first steps in building the bridges that will carry us beyond familiar and often stereotyped modes of thinking and reveal new ways of understanding ourselves and our world.

> *Acknowledging and discussing our different, but otherwise unacknowledged, subject positions are essential first steps in building the bridges that will carry us beyond familiar and often stereotyped modes of thinking and reveal new ways of understanding ourselves and our world.*

It is never easy, within an institutional culture that prizes conformity, to own our status as outsiders, regardless of the source of our difference or alienation. When we do so, we risk cutting ourselves off from any institutional authority we may hold—and from the power and protection that this authority, however limited it may be, confers. The poet and visionary, William Blake[7] reminds us that, "The cut worm forgives the plow" (p. 89). By cutting through our socially constructed public identities as academic and institutional authorities—roles that mask essential dimensions of our personal identities, constrain our pedagogy, and stifle our creativity—we open ourselves up to the possibility of regeneration, to the opportunity to build new selves that we can own more fully and honestly. This, in turn, enables and empowers us to model for our students new ways of understanding—and of reshaping—themselves and their world. This, indeed, is the work of Transformative Learning.

J. DAVID MACEY

J. David Macey is Professor of English at the University of Central Oklahoma, where he also served as an Assistant Vice President in the Office of Academic Affairs, coordinating a range of initiatives in the areas of diversity and globalization, and as a faculty advisor to the university's LGBTQ+ student alliance. A graduate of Yale, Brown, and Vanderbilt Universities, he teaches a wide range of courses in literature, writing, and the history of the English language. He is the coeditor, with Hans Ostrom of the University of Puget Sound, of the five-volume *Greenwood Encyclopedia of African American Literature*, and he has published essays and presented papers on topics including Utopian fiction, the adaptation of Classical motifs in Renaissance poetry, the representation of sexuality and gender in literature and film, and the history of Oklahoma's LGBTQ+ community. In 2006, Macey received the Neely Excellence in Teaching award.

20 CHAPTER TWENTY

J. Kole Kleeman, Ph.D.

On Being a Cross-Cultural Learner in Poland

Being selected as a Fulbright Professor to teach in the Department of American Studies and Mass Media at the University of Lodz, Poland, for the 2015-2016 academic year was one of the most transformative experiences of my academic career. In this essay I would like to share what I have learned about the Fulbright application process, the experience of living and teaching in Poland for a year, and how I learned I was not only a *teacher*, but simultaneously a *learner*, as I encountered a multiplicity of cultural differences within both the Polish higher education system and Polish culture. Finally, I offer some tips for both students and faculty who wish to take the opportunity to live abroad and to further their global and cultural competencies.

The Fulbright Application Process

The Fulbright website is www.cies.org. After studying the site, I decided I would best be a candidate for a Core Fulbright teaching specialist application in Eastern Europe. I contacted a friend from Washington D.C. who has been a Fulbright reviewer and has had two awards. I explained I was very interested in Poland and he encouraged, giving me tips on developing my project statement and "tagging" it. Tagging is where you can easily be located in the system. According to my Fulbright reviewer from Washington, D.C., the system has so many applicants that tagging your vita and project statement will make your identification within the system much easier for the people in charge of ranking potential candidates. For instance, my referee and former Fulbright reviewer had me simply tag my vita with *J. Kole Kleeman, Fulbright Application page 1* at the top of the page. Another important part of tagging was naming the project statement. I titled mine: Transatlantic Media Studies: An Intercultural Exchange of Ideas. Then I listed my teaching expertise and how it connects with the American Studies and Mass Media M.A. program and the GEMMA (Women's and Gender Studies Program). This involved my curriculum development, research and teaching awards. The candidate needs to show s/he is a good match for the host institution.

First, it is imperative the prospective candidate find an institution which is interested and willing to act as host. That task alone is time-consuming. It can take quite a bit of labor writing to the various schools that you think might have a program fitting your specific abilities. Describing your specific interests and academic goals (in *English* and from *your* cultural background) and asking/hoping that your prospective host school clearly understands your interests and goals (in *their* native language and from *their* cultural perspective) will teach you volumes about international communication. It was my experience that naming conventions for Polish academic disciplines—even course descriptions—were perfectly suited to Polish academia and yet could be a struggle for me to understand. For instance, is the department of philology equivalent to communication? (Yes and no, as I found out.) Would teaching in a pedagogical school that has culture and communication be a good fit? A pedagogical school would be a School of Education which is not really my background. I determined that American Studies and Mass Media seemed to fit me best, with an emphasis on popular culture and gender studies.

Sometimes, as I wrote detailed letters describing my teaching and research, I heard nothing back. I spent many months writing to schools. I knew that getting a letter of invitation would only increase my chances of being selected by the Polish-American Fulbright Commission. The American Fulbright Commission in D.C. highly recommended a letter of invitation from the Host Institution.

It Finally Happened

I had written a letter of interest to the University of Lodz about a Fulbright in what, at the time, was called the department of "Transatlantic and Media Studies." The letter was sent to the admissions office, since I did not yet have an email address to the department; that letter was forwarded to the Director dr. hab. Elzbieta Oleksy. (The hab. or habilitation is a government licensure to be awarded tenure and the rank of Associate or Full Professor. In some cases of distinguished academic merit, the President of Poland will make the habilitation award.)

Professor Oleksy said she would forward my interest to Wieslaw Oleksy who had handled potential Fulbright's before. Little did I know I would be the 20th Fulbright recipient in the M.A. program in American Studies and Mass Media. When I eventually received an email response, I rushed back with a "thank you" to the Director, referring to her as "Elizabeth" instead of her correct name, Elzbieta. She wrote me right back saying, "Professor Kleeman we have gotten off to a wretched start; my name is Elzbieta *not* Elizabeth." I even misspelled her husband's name who ended up doing everything to get me over there! I wrote back a very apologetic letter saying this is why we are called "ugly Americans" as we are viewed by Europeans, or in establishing other international relationships. She placed a funny face at the end of her "scolding," letting me know she was forgiving my faux pas.

Next, I began lengthy correspondence with Wieslaw. He offered me the opportunity to teach in the prestigious (GEMMA) Women's and Gender Studies program associated with seven universities in the European Union (EU) and to teach in their M.A. program in American Studies and Mass Media. They liked my courses and with some minor adjustments, the courses fit well into their program.

The Oleksy's are internationally known academics. Elzbieta started the first Women's Studies Center in Poland in 1992. (Remember, Poland only gained emancipation from the Soviet sphere of influence in 1989.) She was the Inaugural Dean of the new Faculty of International Relations and Political Science bringing very progressive voices to the ongoing struggles for human rights in Poland and in the European Union.

Arrival

I arrived in Warsaw on September 15, 2015. I was greeted by a younger professor in the department, Dr. Marek Wojtazek. I took three suitcases full of clothes, books and DVD's for my teaching materials. Marek was a splendid person. In the previous year, he had a Fulbright to the University of Illinois. We had a cup of coffee before the cab came to transport me from Warsaw to Lodz with all of my luggage. The cab was to take me to Wierzbowa 6 A/B which would be my apartment for 11 months. I was dropped off at this older, brick building which was Soviet-style architecture when the Poles lived under the sphere of Soviet influence from 1945–1989. Before Communism, the Poles lived under Nazi Occupation from 1939 at the beginning of WWII. You could not help but sense the prior regime's presence—built into the architecture and the architectonics of horror of the Nazi invasion. My first visit to the Jewish Memorial and Cemetery, very close to where I was living, was used as a major transportation hub for the deportation of the Jews to the most notorious of camps, Auschwitz-Birkenau and others. I witnessed the tiny rail cars with barbed windows where the Jews were caged on the way to most certain death. This was truly a transformational learning experience to see the horrors of the strong arm of Nazism first-hand.

Marek, my Fulbright shepherd and the person with whom I shared an office, took me on this first tour.

A Fulbright shepherd is necessary when living in a foreign country. Marek was indispensable in helping me navigate the trams, putting my syllabus online for my courses, and generally adjusting to the shock of living in another culture. Wiesiek was also very helpful in setting me up in my apartment, which he and Elzbieta owned. Every day was a new learning experience.

I learned what life was like under the Communist era in Poland. Polish people like helping each other, since they had to under Soviet rule. Polish people celebrate their "name day" as it falls on the calendar. This involves sharing food at the office or home—especially sweets—as they are very much a part of Polish culture. Another cultural ritual I observed was "Day of the Dead" on November 1st and "All Souls Day" on November 2nd. This was a very meaningful holiday to Polish people where they place candles and flowers on graves and speak to their loved ones who have died. It is a huge commemorative ceremonial ritual. Early on in my stay, I got to participate in "The Festival of Lights" on Piotrkowska Street, the main street in Lodz, where all the restaurants and pubs are found. This was a large and beautiful celebration; Marek, my shepherd, took me. I felt somewhat nervous with the enormous crowds of people. People came from all over Poland to the event. After about three weeks in Lodz, I pronounced the main street "Piotrkowska" as "Perestroikia" to my host who helped me get there, Wiesiek Oleksy. He screamed at me, and understandably so, since Perestroikia means Soviet restructuring during the 1980s. Polish people do not have any fondness toward the Russians. Again, I was an ugly American.

Teaching in Poland

Polish higher education differs greatly in comparison to the U.S. system. For one, higher education is free to Polish citizens. Course offerings are similar to ours, in that the curriculum is internationalized with a lot of mobility or exchange students such as I taught in the GEMMA (Women's and Gender Studies) program. American Studies and Mass Media was both a B.A. and M.A. program. Students often take 8-12 courses at once. School began October 1st and ended after Christmas. The second semester is called Summer Semester beginning in January. I was assigned to teach my Media Studies seminar to M.A. students in the department and Representations of Gays and Lesbians to 2nd year GEMMA students completing their mobility requirements. The Directors of the program, Elzbieta and Wieslaw, felt strongly that students should be taught the American professors' own courses. The department was renamed American Studies and Mass Media. The students loved learning about American culture and media, and the gay and lesbian social movements in the United States and Germany. As Marek explained to me, you give the students a short syllabi and then the course objectives go to administration.

There weren't many books available to students so I had to scan the reading materials I brought. The students were very fluent in English, in fact, the entire program was taught in English. My students would help me out with the pronunciation of their names, such as Milkołaj Czerwinski, by having me refer to him simply as Mick.

> *Although Polish students are very reserved compared to Americans, I found they would be open to critical discussion after time spent with me in the classroom. Indeed, they were more than eager to discuss their knowledge of American culture and mass media.*

The courses only met once per week for 1 hour and 50 minutes. I was told by my Fulbright host that I could cover only about 70% of what I do in my regular courses in the states. I was told that "lecture" was the way to deliver information. Although Polish students are very reserved compared to Americans, I found they would be open to critical discussion after time spent with me in the classroom. Indeed, they were more than eager to discuss their knowledge of American culture and mass media.

The GEMMA students I taught the first semester were in their 2nd year before completing their master's thesis. They were a joy to teach. They were already ensconced in the subject matter as second year students. They were required as part of their program to have "mobility" or to complete one semester with a participating institution in the E.U. I had students that semester from Serbia, Spain, Germany, and Nepal; all very interested in human rights based upon sex, gender and sexual orientation. Many GEMMA students came from countries where women, lesbians, and gay men had very few rights. One of my Spanish GEMMA students was working to improve the plight of LGBTQ+ people in Ghana. Some of these special students would go on to earn a Ph.D. and become academics. Others were given the tools to enable global activism.

I was always a learner in my courses, listening about where the students came from and the geo-political environments of which I had very little knowledge. Many of the Polish students I taught were going to the U.S. or wanted me to help them get here. Poland lacks economic opportunities; many of my students worked in England (until Brexit) and in Ireland.

Politics

I arrived in Poland shortly before the nation's election for Prime Minister. The liberal party had become too relaxed and the far-right "Law and Justice" party was voted into power. Many of the academics at the University were organizing protests. I also saw protests for the conservative side. There was some discussion at the University about the developing state-sanctioned media. In fact, when President Obama was attending the NATO Summit in Warsaw on July 8, 2016, he admonished the Polish government for censoring the news. Of course, his comments were never placed in the news. The American Ambassador to Poland, Paul W. Jones, visited our department and gave a lecture on US-Polish relations. It was nice to meet these diplomats and gain an overview of embassy responsibilities.

> *The American Ambassador to Poland, Paul W. Jones, visited our department and gave a lecture on US-Polish relations. It was nice to meet these diplomats and gain an overview of embassy responsibilities.*

I was interviewed by the local television media twice. The first time about gun control in the United States and the second about Hillary Clinton the day she was nominated by the Electoral College for president.

University politics were different than in the U.S. higher education system. There were nominations for a new Dean of the faculty of Political Science and International Relations. One of the candidates running was from the American Studies and Mass Media department. It appeared—on the surface—to be a very democratic process, with students, staff, and faculty all voting. I remember my students were heavily involved, attending speeches the candidates were giving. I also heard all kinds of stories about swaying different constituencies to vote in a certain way—politics on campus.

Networking

As I previously mentioned, the Polish people enjoy helping each other out, especially after surviving life under Communism. My hosts and colleagues became invaluable resources to me. Wiesiek Oleksy made a contact for me to give a seminar at the University of Grenada, Spain. Marek provided me with several books and articles on what he calls "digitization." I taught a new course here at UCO on International Media Studies in the fall semester 2016. Marek gave me a plethora of new publications for the new course.

I gathered from interviews and observations of faculty that some of the success of the program was due to team research and collaborations over international conferences. Professors in Poland have heavy teaching and research loads. The sense of unity in the department was strong, something I was pleased to observe. I did not observe factions, bullying or any such behaviors, but rather a strong network of scholars working together.

I also met some Ph.D. students who were doing their research in Poland and were awarded Fulbright's. Another larger group were the English Teaching Assistants (ETA's) who were provided dormitory housing and worked with students on their writing and speaking skills. This would be a good opportunity for undergraduate students to engage with another culture.

Transformative Practices Learned Upon Returning to UCO

I share with my Intro to Human Communication courses, and my newly developed seminar in International Communication, a number of tips and techniques that I gained from living in Poland for a full year of cultural immersion. I stress the importance of correct pronunciation of names and places. As I learned the hard way, this can be insulting to the people who you will be working closely with. It is also important to study the geo-politics of where you are going to live. For instance, Poland is 98% Catholic. This helps the prospective resident to become familiar with the cultural mores and norms of the culture. Also knowing some history of the cultural trauma Poland went through being the first country to be invaded by the Nazi party in WWII, then under the Soviet Regime. I went to Auschwitz-Birkenau and saw first-hand the evil of this period. I show my students the room full of hair where furniture was made from human bodies. When I teach about the Gay and Lesbian Holocaust in Germany, I was fortunate to visit Berlin and see in museums all the groups the Nazis designated for elimination. Berlin doesn't have any prohibitions about taking pictures inside their monumental repositories of museums. In this way, from being there, I can communicate my experience in much greater visual detail to my students.

Conclusion

In this essay, I have tried to offer some tips for faculty and students interested in applying for a Fulbright Scholarship. It requires genuine motivation on the part of the applicant. The American Fulbright Commission in Washington, D.C., is very helpful, and I simply cannot say enough good things about the Polish-American Fulbright Commission. Investigating the culture you are going to live in is of the utmost importance, including basic pronunciation of names and greetings. Studying the geo-politics of the region will be most helpful for understanding the culture in which you are going to live.

Should you make the decision, you will be transformed from learning about the multiplicity of cultural differences. It can lead—as it has for me—to a window of future opportunity. My teaching in our Gender and Sexuality Studies Minor, Intro to Human Communication courses, and my new course in International Media Studies, have all been fortified by what I learned in this journey of transformational learning.

J. KOLE KLEEMAN

J. Kole Kleeman, Ph.D. (Ohio University) serves as Professor Emeritus of Mass Communication and Director of the Media Studies minor at UCO. He has published on a wide range of topics including masculinity and violence in the media, hate crimes in the media, media literacy and anti-violence education in the media, and recently a book chapter on advertising in the 1960s. Kleeman is also an affiliate faculty member for the new Gender and Sexuality Studies minor at UCO. His work with the GEMMA (Women's and Gender Studies) program in Poland has helped to fortify his teaching and research interest in UCO's new minor. Kleeman won a faculty merit award for excellence in teaching in 2003. In 2007, Kleeman received the Neely Excellence in Teaching award.

21 CHAPTER TWENTY-ONE

Gloria Caddell, Ph.D.

Roots, Branches, Flowers, Fruits, and Seeds: My Transformation into a Botanist and Teacher

As a botanist, I often use analogies from plants to describe processes, and I believe the way a tree grows and develops best describes my growth and development as a learner, teacher, and scientist. When a seed germinates, the first part of the embryo to emerge is the radicle, which develops into the root system. My "roots" are the people who first helped me to become established as a seedling and continue to sustain me. For example, my mother was my "primary root" who, as a Girl Scout leader, took me on long hikes and inspired me to pursue a career that allowed me to spend significant amounts of time outdoors. I remember her talking to me about going to college even before I went to first grade! Another "root" was my high school biology teacher who required me to observe and document every change taking place each day in an outdoor plot on campus. This forever influenced me to pay attention to, and appreciate, the details of the world around me. As I grew, additional "roots" provided support for me. My master's advisor, C. Earle Smith, Jr., with Ph.D.'s in both biology and anthropology, provided opportunities for me to participate in large-scale and collaborative archaeological projects, influencing how I later incorporated research into the biology classes I taught. My Ph.D. advisor, Clifford Parks, provided the opportunity for me to immerse myself in Japanese culture for two and a half years while I conducted my dissertation research on the population genetics and pollination ecology of camellia.

The stem of a tree—the trunk—grows taller each year, and branches develop. The branches and twigs represent the various pathways my life has taken, and leaves represent the experiences I have had and the multitude of things I have learned. Some branches are longer and wider than others, symbolizing the major and minor pathways of my life and how much I gained from exposure to great teachers, different cultures, and various methods of exploration and inquiry. Some branches on a tree, particularly the lower branches, "self-prune" or fall off. These represent earlier pathways of my life, such as my involvement in orchestra in high school. Although what is left of these branches might appear to be only scars on a trunk, the leaves on those branches at one time captured solar energy and synthesized organic compounds that contributed to the increase in girth of the trunk—i.e. an annual ring of wood produced each year, as well as an increase in the thickness of the bark. My "trunk" grew stronger each year, and those experiences still contribute to who I am and how I learn and teach. As annual ring width varies year to year on a tree, depending on availability of resources, so has the growth of my "trunk" varied. Some years are more stressful for a tree, the same as in my life. About fifteen years ago, I was diagnosed with a vocal cord disorder called spasmodic dysphonia that threatened my ability to continue teaching in the classroom. During that time, my trunk might not have grown quite so tall, but it thickened. The trunks of trees exposed to high levels of stress (think of stunted trees on a wind-swept cliff or at tree line on a mountain) often grow larger in diameter, and likewise, I believe that my stressful years have contributed to my strength and resilience as a teacher and individual. One of the "largest branches" on my tree is the many years that I have spent in the classroom, lab, and field, teaching botany, plant taxonomy, plant ecology, environmental biology, pollination biology and research classes at UCO. Another "branch" is the time I have spent with students over the past fifteen years, documenting the incredible native plant communities occurring on gypsum outcrops in northwestern Oklahoma. My "tree" has grown tall and strong, with a branching pattern like no other.

When trees reach a certain level of maturity, they can produce flowers, and these are analogous to my students, who I try to nourish through encouragement and mentorship like a tree nourishes its flowers. All of my experiences have influenced the way I teach, interact with, and try to transform students. Because I learned at a young age that the outdoors was not something to fear, I want my students to also feel comfortable in it. I have a passion for helping students notice the world around them, and I tirelessly work to increase their powers of observation. Although many students are "visual" learners, most students come into plant biology classes unaware that they are suffering from "plant blindness." They do not have well-developed powers of observation. "Plant blindness," as described by Wandersee and Schussler,[1] is "the inability to see or notice the plants in one's own environment." This leads to "an inability to recognize the importance of plants in the biosphere and human affairs," and "an inability to appreciate [their] aesthetic and

> *I have a passion for helping students notice the world around them, and I tirelessly work to increase their powers of observation.*

unique biological features." To become scientists, students must first learn to observe. Few students know which plants grow in their own backyards, and increasingly, most have little outdoor experience. I try to increase my students' powers of observation and their appreciation of plants by taking them on field trips to the campus gardens, to local parks, and to natural areas across Oklahoma. I constantly encourage them to notice the daily changes in the natural world around them, from tiny wind-pollinated flowers in the spring to the development of winter buds. I provide them with hand lenses so they can see the tiny star-shaped hairs on post oak leaves, the rusty hairs on red elm buds, and the intricate details of grass flowers. I am delighted (though also a little worried) when my students tell me that they can't keep their eyes on the road as they drive because they are looking at roadside plants. Isaac Newton said, "If I have ever made any valuable discoveries, it has been owing more to patient attention, than to any other talent."

Although my students will not all have careers in botany, I trust the observation skills I help them develop might lead them to make valuable discoveries in whatever field they choose. I want the knowledge they acquire in my classes to enhance enjoyment of their daily lives and to develop in them a sense of responsibility to conserve the natural world. I feel so lucky to have been in the presence of native azaleas covering the slopes of the Japanese mountains, tiny orchids clinging to the trees of the Amazon forest, ground-hugging plants of the alpine tundra of Yellowstone, ancient bristlecone pine trees next to a glacier in Nevada (and ancient post oak trees in the Cross Timbers of Oklahoma!), towering coast redwood trees in the temperate rainforests of the West Coast, and the plants and pollinators of the prairie and the gypsum outcrops of northwestern Oklahoma. I want my students to be able to explore such places and understand and appreciate what they see. How satisfying it is to receive emails from former students who send me pictures of a tropical rainforest they have visited, tell me how they went hiking and were able to identify the plants along the trail, or tell me that I inspired them to plant their first garden or grow their own flowers for their wedding! And even more satisfying was attending the wedding of one of my graduate students at the base of a gypsum mesa on her research site in northwestern Oklahoma! Additionally, my concept of "students" has broadened to include the campus community and the public. My students are all those who walk across campus and see the names of the plants on signs I helped post as a member of the campus landscape task force, who use a pamphlet I've prepared on the flora of a state park, who attend the field trips I lead for professional and community organizations, and even the students of the teachers who participate in the teachers' workshops I have led on the flora, landscape, and environmental issues of Oklahoma.

Early in my career, I worked as an archaeological botanist in the field and lab alongside colleagues who were carefully analyzing animal remains, stone tools, pottery, etc. Together we pieced together a coherent picture of what life was like thousands of years ago at the sites we excavated. Realizing the value of such interdisciplinary collaboration and synthesis, I have carried this model into my classes. I try to help students see that their research is significant and part of a much larger picture. For example, in my pollination biology class, each student independently conducts field research on a prairie plant species. But as they share their findings with students investigating other species at the same field site, they gain a broad understanding of the evolution of diverse pollination strategies. They see that different plants have quite different strategies for surviving, attracting pollinators, and producing offspring. In my introductory botany class, I have had groups of students design experiments to test the effects of a plant hormone on particular aspects of growth and development of a plant species. Because different groups test different effects in different plants, the students see that there are multiple effects of the same hormone and that the effects can differ depending on which plant species is being used. And, I always encourage them to test the effect on a plant in which the effect of that hormone has not been studied, or on an aspect of growth and development that has not been studied. Similar to my work in archaeological botany, when we were asking questions about a culture to which no one knew the answers (and we never knew what the next shovel full of dirt was going to turn up!), the students are asking questions that no one has answered. Likewise, in my pollination biology class, students often study plant species for which the pollination ecology has never been documented. To develop into professional scientists, students need to ask meaningful questions that explore beyond what is known. I am convinced that students learn best when they seek answers to questions they pose themselves, and the best questions are those for which no one yet knows the answer. The best measure of success in my classroom is when students ask me questions I can't answer, and in fact,

> *I am convinced that students learn best when they seek answers to questions they pose themselves, and the best questions are those for which no one yet knows the answer.*

sometimes no one has yet answered. This means that I have stimulated them to think a little more deeply about what they have seen and heard in my classroom, and I hope that one day they will contribute to science by seeking the answers to the questions they pose.

My experiences have also affected the way I interact with, encourage, and mentor students. I was a rather shy college student and reticent to speak out in class, but Dr. Smith recognized my potential and took me under his wing. He allowed me to assist him with the identification of archaeological plant remains from sites in South, Central and North America, encouraged me to present my first talk at a scientific meeting as an undergraduate, and helped me develop confidence. I wonder where I would be today if he had not approached me and allowed me to do research with him. I try to "pay this forward" by approaching students myself to let them know the potential I see in them. Also, spending two and a half years as a research student in Japan gave me an understanding of what it is like to get off the airplane in a strange country and feel in many ways like a small child, learning how to do basic things in a different way in a new culture, and living through embarrassing mistakes I made when speaking and writing. As the only American at my university, and as a member of a community of international students, I became interested in other countries because I was friends with students from those countries. By gaining knowledge of a very different culture, I developed an entirely different perspective on my own country. I came to see travel not only as a luxury but as an education, and to realize that an understanding and consideration of others' views is a necessity in our global environment. My experiences have certainly made me more patient and empathetic with the international students in my classes as they struggle like I did to learn how to navigate college life in a different culture. My experiences in Japan also influenced how I mentor students. I was there before the age of the internet, and communication with my Ph.D. advisor in the U.S. was only by "snail" mail, so I was forced to become an independent thinker and researcher. Because of what I gained from that experience, I have tried to provide my students constructive guidance, but avoid nonconstructive "handholding." I have immersed myself as much as possible in my students' projects so that I can model how to do research. I have often become so interested in their research that I find myself doing things like helping a student set cave cricket traps at various distances and in various directions around cave entrances in northwestern Oklahoma to see how far the crickets ventured out at night. But it has been a constant challenge to remind myself that these are primarily the *students'* projects and *their* responsibility, and my role is to help the *students themselves* gain the skills to become independent researchers.

My experiences with my disability have also affected the way I interact with students. My symptoms of spasmodic dysphonia appeared when I was teaching one summer. Nerves were causing an overcontraction of my vocal cord muscles, resulting in a "strangled" voice. I was determined to keep teaching, but it took several months to get an accurate diagnosis and begin to receive Botox injections to relax the muscles. I will never forget the understanding and patience my students showed me during that period, and I try to show the same level of understanding and patience to my own students who are struggling with anything in their lives. I have not let this disability define who I am, and I do not let a disability define a student who is challenged by one.

Not all flowers will produce fruits, but many do. The seeds contained within are those students who I have inspired the most—not just those who have pursued a career in science, but also, those whose lives have been positively changed by being shown how to observe, understand, and appreciate the daily changes in the natural world around them, and advocate for the conservation of the natural world. They are the next "trees" of the forest, each with its own unique branching pattern.

GLORIA CADDELL

Dr. Gloria Caddell grew up camping, hiking and canoeing in the pine and swamp forests of southern Alabama and taking long walks on Gulf Coast beaches. These experiences sparked an interest in nature and inspired her to pursue a career in science. Her B.A. and M.A. degrees are in anthropology from the University of Alabama, where she specialized in the analysis of archaeological plant remains. She earned a Ph.D. in biology from the University of North Carolina at Chapel Hill. Her dissertation, on the population genetics and pollination of camellia, is based on research she conducted in Japan. She has taught biology at UCO since 1990, chaired the Department of Biology, and is currently the Associate Dean of the College of Mathematics and Science. She does research on the flora of Oklahoma, particularly the flora of gypsum outcrops of northwestern Oklahoma, and the pollination of Oklahoma prairie plants. In 2010, Caddell received the Neely Excellence in Teaching award.

22

CHAPTER
TWENTY-TWO

Luis Montes, Ph.D.

Take the Next Step: Opportunities for Growth

The Quiet Observer: Finding a Path

Ononeof the hardest things I have done was to start graduate school in a new place, ten hours away from family and friends. Growing up the third of four children, with only six years separating the oldest and youngest, I experienced all kinds of interactions with my siblings. There were the expected competitions for attention, the always-changing alliances among the four of us, but also many examples of teamwork and mutual support. As the third child, I had examples and paths I could follow. This made some paths smoother, but it also had its drawbacks. On the first day of class, teachers would ask if I was the younger brother of my two very talented older siblings. I realized that while my path may have been smoother, there were expectations based on what my siblings had done. I learned that in order to get out from the shadow of my older siblings I had to try things they had not pursued. When it came time to select a musical direction in sixth grade, I decided to learn to play violin, whereas my sister and brother had chosen choir. While they ended their musical pursuits in junior high school, I continued with the violin through high school, and ended up teaching myself guitar as well.

I was always the most introverted of my siblings. While they would be very talkative during dinner each night, I would slowly eat my food and keep up with the two or three conversations going on around the table. My siblings had a lot to say. I enjoyed listening to and learning from them, trying to process and understand everything that was going on. This tendency to listen and process carried over to other parts of my life as well. Although I generally did well in my classes, I was certainly not the first one to volunteer answers or speak up in class. When I was in Boy Scouts with my older brother, he was always one of the leaders in the troop while I would take on some minor service role. Because he was my older brother, I knew he understood things and would know what was needed in a given situation. As my brother and other scouts would be planning meetings or outings, I would be listening and taking notes. It was during one of these planning discussions that I had one of my early self-discoveries. While planning an event, the troop leaders had reached some impasse and could not seem to solve the problem. While the solution seemed obvious to me, I was not used to having to speak up because somebody else would usually come up with the solution. But as the discussion continued, nothing was getting resolved. Finally, and unexpectedly, I spoke up and presented what I thought was a resolution to the problem. Perhaps because I rarely spoke up, everyone was willing to listen to my suggestion. However, what had the most impact on me was when my older brother affirmed that my solution would work and that it was a creative way to solve the problem. Especially when you are competing with an older brother for attention, it can be very meaningful when he recognizes your talents. This gave me confidence to take on greater leadership responsibilities in the troop, including serving in the top leadership position in the troop for two years—after my older brother had left the troop, of course.

Since I was closest in age to my older brother, I followed in his path academically. He took a lot of science and math classes in high school, so I did as well. While he chose physics as a major in college, I chose chemistry as my major a few years later. At that point our academic paths began to diverge. While he spent a lot of his time on his coursework and excelled as a physics and math double major, I ended up spending more time in chemistry club and student government and double majored in chemistry and philosophy. During my time in the chemistry club, I discovered what I wanted to do with my life: teach chemistry to college students.

The General Chemistry classes at my university had common exams on a few Wednesdays during the semester. The members of the chemistry club would hold review and study sessions for two evenings before the common exams. As a member and officer of the chemistry club, I participated in these help sessions and discovered that I enjoyed explaining chemistry to other students. I appreciated the logic of the discipline and enjoyed the challenge of getting another person to understand the organization of chemical knowledge. I found it an intriguing puzzle to alter my explanations based on what each individual student understood. I now knew I wanted to be involved with chemistry as a discipline, and I knew what I wanted to teach in the discipline. After talking to a few of my chemistry professors, I learned that in order to teach at the university level I would need to get an advanced chemistry degree. Fortunately, by that time I was familiar with that path, as my older sister had started a graduate program in speech pathology and my older brother had started a Ph.D. program in physics.

My first semester of graduate school was probably my most

difficult transition, as I did not yet have local support networks as I did back home. I remember spending a few weekends by myself in my apartment, studying for my classes and not talking to another person all weekend. I realized I would need to be more intentional about connecting with other people in order to create new networks. This experience prepared me for later transitions. While in the past I could rely on family or friends for a path to start down, I now realized I could find my own directions when I needed to do so. My graduate school education in chemistry consisted of taking a few courses for each of the first three semesters, and then spending much of the remaining time conducting research and writing up my work. Along with the classwork and lab work, I had the opportunity to serve as a teaching assistant in the undergraduate chemistry laboratories. While this took time away from my research, it gave me time to learn about the practice of teaching at the university level.

During my final year, I worked as an instructor at a local historically black college, teaching a general chemistry lecture for a small number of students. A few weeks before I was to begin, I was given a copy of the textbook, the names of the students, and a rough schedule of topics that would need to be covered. There was very little guidance on how I was to teach this course. I taught this chemistry course for one year while completing my Ph.D. I then moved on to some temporary teaching positions at another university for about four years. During this time, I grew frustrated with the limited number of courses I was given to teach. I sought out other opportunities at nearby universities, hoping to get a more permanent position teaching more classes. I also began considering alternative careers and started looking into preparing for law school. However, my efforts making contact with other universities eventually paid off, as one of them contacted me about an opening. After going through the application process, I received an offer for a tenure-track position at a primarily undergraduate institution—the University of Central Oklahoma. I accepted this position and was assigned a typical schedule of two lecture and two lab sections. The work also included some expectation of scholarly activity, as well as a service component that required me to participate in committee work at the department, college, and university levels.

Breaking New Ground

Reflecting on my education, it was clear that my undergraduate and graduate chemistry degrees had prepared me for doing chemistry, or for the scholarly part of my new job expectations. However, I had very little formal training in how to teach a class or how to work on committees. I imagine that this situation happens to many of us. We have been specifically prepared to do parts of our jobs, but we have to learn other aspects of our jobs as we go. How do we learn to do these things? We jump in and try things. We use what limited experiences we may have in similar situations and apply them to our current situations. We may use the examples of other people we have seen in such situations and may follow in those paths. In my experiences in my family, I have always been an observer of interactions between people, so I relied on what I had observed other people doing as a starting point. I based my initial approach to teaching on the way I had been taught. For my service responsibilities, I relied on my experiences in extracurricular activities. I had held service and leadership roles in Boy Scouts, as well as in the Chemistry Club and student government while working on my undergraduate degree. I used my observations of other leaders in those groups as a model for my university service.

> *If we only do what we have seen others do, we will never do things in new ways, or improve upon how things are done. It is important to add our personal insights to how we do things.*

If we only do what we have seen others do, we will never do things in new ways, or improve upon how things are done. It is important to add our personal insights to how we do things. I have found that a little bit of reflection can help me understand what skills and talents I have and how I can apply them to new situations. My skills in observing people were at first helpful while working in groups around the university. I learned to pay attention to what other people were saying in order to better understand what was important to them. It also helped me think about the goals of the service activities I engaged with, as well as to realize that the social component of committee work—valuing people—is equally as important as the work product of the group. I could also apply these skills to my work in the classroom. Rather than focusing on what I was presenting to my students, I learned to pay attention to what the students were understanding and where they were struggling. This resulted in significant changes in the way I structured and taught my courses. I had to think about the purpose of my teaching, and how what I did in and out of the classroom impacted students. I created space in my teaching to listen to my students. This gave me a chance to hear what they were thinking and to assess how well they understood the class material. In addition to my skills in observing people, my chemistry and philosophy courses gave me extensive experience in using logic and drawing conclusions from evidence. I have used these skills throughout my work life. They helped me structure my courses and committee work in ways that make sense.

After I had been in a tenure-track position for a few years, I had a pretty good handle on how my courses would go. I had made good progress in my service work and held some faculty leadership roles at the university level. I also had a few publications. However, I knew that I had more to learn. This was reminiscent of my experiences growing up. I would start off on paths that others had paved before me, but along the way I would find new directions to go. Although I appreciate the work of those who have gone before me, I tend to become dissatisfied if I continue to do the same thing year after year. This is kind of an inquisitive dissatisfaction—a curiosity about how to improve upon what I am currently doing and an interest in finding out what else is out there for me to do. This inquisitive dissatisfaction has driven me to reflect on the talents and skills I have. It has been a reminder to ask myself how I can improve upon whatever it is I am doing. I have been working in universities for over twenty years, but I still have more to learn. This inquisitive dissatisfaction drives me to seek opportunities to better understand higher education and student learning. It has broadened my reading beyond the chemical literature, and it has pushed me to interact with more people from across my institution and beyond.

> *I have been working in universities for over twenty years, but I still have more to learn. This inquisitive dissatisfaction drives me to seek opportunities to better understand higher education and student learning. It has broadened my reading beyond the chemical literature, and it has pushed me to interact with more people from across my institution and beyond.*

Continuing the Journey

None of us graduate from college as a finished product. Hopefully, whatever we have learned in college will start us on a path that we find productive and fulfilling. But it is important to remember that it is still a path. It is long, it may have detours, and you may end up headed to a destination you did not initially intend, but it is still a path. How will you travel that path? What resources will you bring with you as you travel that path? Will you be open to new possibilities you encounter along that path? I found it productive to start on paths others had traveled before me. I was able to think about what I had learned from them. I was able to see where they were and consider if that would be an interesting place for me. Along the way I came across adventures that others never encountered or that I would need to experience for my own growth. I took time to reflect on what I learned from those adventures. I considered what skills and talents I demonstrated during these adventures. When I came to new challenges, I was able to draw upon these demonstrated talents and skills. As I travel my path, I am always asking myself whether there are other ways to get to where I want to go or ways to improve the path for others coming behind me.

When I was growing up, I never would have imagined that I would be doing what I am now. As a relatively quiet student, I would not have thought I would be in front of students teaching a class or taking leadership roles in my work. However, by observing other people, understanding my own talents and skills, and looking for ways to improve, I found myself on a path that is challenging and fulfilling and gives me opportunities to continue my own growth while helping other people.

LUIS MONTES

Luis Montes is a professor and department chair in the Department of Chemistry at the University of Central Oklahoma (UCO). He joined UCO in August 2000 after spending four years in various contingent faculty roles at Oklahoma State University. He earned both a B.S. in Chemistry and a B.A. in Philosophy from New Mexico State University, and a Ph.D. in Chemistry from the University of Texas at Austin. His scholarly pursuits include chemical education and the history and philosophy of chemistry. He applies these to his teaching by helping chemistry majors understand the broader impacts of chemists in society, both historically and currently. His two terms as President of the UCO Faculty Senate inspired him to learn more about how universities function, and as a result he has served as a peer reviewer for the Higher Learning Commission since 2013. Luis enjoys travel, including visiting chemically important sites when possible.

23 CHAPTER TWENTY-THREE

Laura Bolf-Beliveau, Ph.D.

The Transformational Nature of Emotions and Education

A student sits in a first-year composition course as the professor shows a trailer for *Bloody Cartoons*, a documentary about Danish caricatures of Muhammad and the subsequent anger that erupted as Muslims protested around the world. Before the trailer ends, this student gathers his belongings and leaves. The rest of the students look at the professor who merely shrugs and continues with class. The student does not come back the next class session. When the professor finally communicates with him, she discovers that he is just out of the Marines and still has shrapnel in his leg from a battle in Fallujah. Images from the trailer triggered his post-traumatic stress, and he left class, went to his car, and called his VA counselor.

An international graduate student regularly cries in a teaching methods course. She is struggling with reading, writing, and acting out Shakespearean plays. Other students take turns mentoring her. They sit next to her, walk with her after class, email her with support. When she finally seeks out her professor, the conversation moves from her classroom performance to her young son, left with in-laws overseas. She has not seen him in two years, and her husband tells her that her desire for an American master's degree is the cause of the boy's strife. Her selfishness, according to him, is ruining her son's life and their marriage. She wants to maintain an A average to prove that her decision was not worthless.

A male student taking a feminist literature course moves violently in his seat and then tosses his book to the floor. Conversation stops. Everyone looks at him. Then he shrugs his shoulders and the discussion starts again. He interrupts others. The professor tries to redirect the conversation, but the student sighs loudly, throws his belongings into his backpack, and leaves, slamming the door. Before the professor can get back to her office, another male student from that class has emailed her, complaining that his peer is ruining the course. He asks her to do something about it.

Two female students quietly cry as their peers talk about the young adult book *Speak*. Like the protagonist from the book, they were both raped as teenagers. The professor had not given any kind of trigger warning about the book's content, and the entire class can feel their anguish. When one bravely speaks, it is not about the rape in the book. Instead, it is about how the protagonist gets the opportunity to confront her rapist, hold a weapon to his throat, and then have a field hockey team *come to her aid. They tell the class that this is not reality. That there is no closure when it comes to sexual assault. Justice, they say, is rarely achieved.*

A Ph.D. candidate, the first in her family to earn a bachelor's and master's degree, sits in a qualitative research class. Students are workshopping each other's first drafts of articles that must, per the course syllabus, be sent for review to tier one journals. Her work is a mixed-methods study, and when her turn finally arrives, the professor does not ask for feedback from the other students. Instead, she tells the Ph.D. candidate to read a sample published article and revise hers. Then, without pausing, the professor takes her draft, tears it into four parts, and throws it in the garbage. Looking around at her peers for support, the Ph.D. candidate discovers that they are all looking down at the table. No one will make eye contact with her.

Alienation. Regret. Anger. Sadness. Frustration. Embarrassment.

Emotions are always present in teaching and learning. What we do with them affects our educational transformation.

Let's start with the last anecdote, the one with the Ph.D. candidate. I was that Ph.D. candidate. That professor was also on my dissertation committee, and she came into my defense with a pronouncement, something to the effect of, "I'm so mad at you. I stayed up to one in the morning reading your dissertation. I didn't think you could use the methodology that way. But don't worry. I found someone else who did the same thing. He's published. I think you could publish this too." First in the research course with this professor, and now at the dissertation defense, I had emotional responses to this woman's actions and words. In the research class, I wasn't merely embarrassed. I also felt disheartened and ashamed. During my dissertation defense, my first emotion was fear, but that turned quickly to anger. How dare she wait until the night before to read my dissertation? Suggest my work was indefensible only to end telling me it was publishable?

Over a decade later, I see that my emotional responses to these experiences had a long-term effect on me. I became less confident, questioned my ability to do any kind of qualitative research, and set my dissertation aside. I began focusing on literary textual analysis, no qualitative research methodology needed.

Ironically, my dissertation studied how first year female English teachers negotiated their emotional responses to students and classroom environments. I still believed in the feminist theory used in that study, so I began using those philosophies to ground my teaching practices. I wanted to provide a space where emotions in education could empower college students. Focusing on breaking binaries and researcher reflexivity, I employed transformative pedagogical practices.

In her ground-breaking feminist study, *Feeling Power: Emotions and Education*, Megan Boler[1] challenges what she calls the pathology of emotions. She argues that emotion is often pitted against reason, and reason is more valued. Reason is also connected to intellect. This binary often labels emotion to a private matter. As that Ph.D. student, I kept my emotional responses to myself, even felt ashamed that I had them.

But Boler makes another important argument about emotions, stating that "In order to name, imagine and materialize a better world, we need an account of how Western discourses of emotion shape our scholarly work, as well as pedagogical recognition of how emotions shape our classroom interactions" (p. xv). If we keep emotions out of the public sphere of the classroom, then their potential as agents of change is lost.

One of the first steps of my transformation as a teacher began with Boler's concept of the Pedagogy of Discomfort. She believes that transformative learning should consider the importance of emotion:

> A pedagogy of discomfort begins by inviting educators and students to engage in critical inquiry regarding values and cherished beliefs, and to examine constructed self-images in relation to how one has learned to perceive others. Within this culture of inquiry and flexibility, a central focus is to recognize how emotions define how and what one chooses to see, and conversely, not to see." (pp. 176-177)

I cannot help but wonder, ten years after my experience in that qualitative research class, if my discomfort was perhaps shared by others in that space. I kept my emotions private, but had I voiced them, made them public, what would have happened? Would that potential discomfort bring forth the examination Boler posits above? Not necessarily. The public statement of how we feel does not necessarily produce transformative learning. Something else needs to be done; the binary of public vs. private

So, emotions are vital to transformative learning. They need a place to go— this third space. Once there, all classroom participants must be reflexive—cognizant of their own beliefs while open to discovery of others.

needs to shift to a third space.

The concept of third space may sound metaphoric—that something is happening in a figurative way, but that's not the case. Think back to that anecdote about the two women who are survivors of sexual assault. Their tears were a display of private emotion. The quiet reaction of their peers, the silence, was a public display. When they provided a testimonial, an explanation of their frustration with the text, that opened up a third space.

Once in that third space, what needs to happen for transformative learning to occur? Here I tie in another aspect of my dissertation research that became part of my teaching pedagogy: reflexivity. Leavy and Harris[2] believe reflexivity in research requires us to be mindful of the "context of discovery." How researchers situate themselves and then interpret their discoveries depends on their own personal, political, biographical, ideological selves (p. 103).

Therefore, to use a third space effectively, teachers must not police that space vis-à-vis their own belief system. Indeed, teachers, like researchers, cannot "disavow our mental or bodily experiences, including our emotions, as they are tools for conducting effective research on sensitive topics"[3] (p. 118). So, emotions are vital to transformative learning. They need a place to go—this third space. Once there, all classroom participants must be reflexive—cognizant of their own beliefs while open to discovery of others.

Let's think back to the opening anecdotes. The first four are from my own experiences as a university professor, and in light of the concepts presented above, here are a few questions for thinking about the efficacy of transformation via emotional experience:

- Why did an emotional third space open?
- Is the third space safe?
- What questions, activities, discussions could inspire reflexivity?
- Does the discussion in third space allow for varying worldviews?

The first situation, the one where the veteran walked out, happened very early in my university teaching career. When he left my first-year composition course, the third space opened and closed simultaneously. A discussion about the documentary seemed too visceral (and untimely) when he returned. Discussing his reaction with him not in the room would have been unconscionable. No activities or discussions seemed workable at this time, so this situation proved only reflexive for me. I realized that I had a different worldview than he, but it wasn't just my lack of military experience. It was also my blindness to the reality of being in the military. I had processed my emotions about the documentary from a safe distance. He did not have that choice. I did learn, however, to think about the content of my courses carefully and to discuss content before showing video clips or assigning certain readings.

I did not share the private conversation I had in my office with the international student to the rest of the class. However, her public display of tears in class did open a third space that felt safe. I could tell this by her willingness to publicly share the difficulties of understanding the course content. Because the majority of the students were practicing teachers or preservice teachers, they wanted to know how they could support students in their own classrooms when those students grew frustrated and wanted to give up. Given the openness of the students, including this international student, I asked questions pertinent to theater-based pedagogy (acting out literature in a non-theater class): Must all students participate? How can activities move from low-stakes to high-stakes and allow students to grow comfortable with the process? How do our own lived experiences affect how we teach? How we learn?

The third space in my feminist literature course was more difficult to negotiate. The concepts discussed were tied to patriarchy, hegemony, and power. The course syllabus included this statement: "These readings were chosen to build spaces of understanding, hopefully across belief systems and lived experiences. All voices are welcome. I hope we will approach these texts and issues with support, kindness, and encouragement. We have so much to learn this semester." Although we discussed this statement and watched Chimamanda Ngozi Adichie's Ted Talk about the danger of a single story on the first day of class, I had not built in reflexive opportunities for the students. Previous sections of this course had activities like developing essential questions for the course in weeks one and two and then referring back to them on the midterm and final exam. I had also built in reflections written privately via the learning management system (D2L) that gave me opportunities to respond to emotional third spaces in ways that were less confrontational. Since teaching that section, I have made those activities mandatory once again. But it would be too simplistic to assume that those adjustments alone would have moved this third space from confrontational to reflexive. Emotions do not always have a simple explanation. Also, time is needed to realize the transformative nature of third space.

Although the sexual assault victims in my young adult literature course were in pain, their willingness to share their experiences opened up a very rich third space, one they later said felt safe. Unlike the situations discussed above where male students walked out, this classroom environment already had begun with reflexive assignments—a self-study of their own reading lives as adolescents. They had also read about the disconnect between adults writing about adolescents and what real adolescents think, do, experience and say. We already had questioned the efficacy of young adult books, current and canonical, and perhaps some work had already been done in breaking of the binary that would position adults vs. adolescents. They were ready to critique the writers of these books and the kinds of messages they made about issues like sexual assault. This third space opened and stayed open for the duration of the semester. Exploring that space was a transformation for us all.

> *...for transformative teaching and learning to take place, participants must do— must engage, debate, listen, speak, think, etc. Active engagement within a third space can produce effects that move classrooms from passive to active.*

Previously in this chapter, I stated that emotions are always present in teaching and learning. What we **do** with them affects our educational transformation. "Do" is the important word in this claim: for transformative teaching and learning to take place, participants must do—must engage, debate, listen, speak, think, etc. Active engagement within a third space can produce effects that move classrooms from passive to active.

Some may argue that emotions are absent in their classrooms, that, perhaps, there is no room for emotional displays of any kind. But it is highly unlikely that emotions are truly absent—perhaps they have been relegated to the binaries discussed by Boler: reason vs. emotion and public vs. private. In both binaries, emotion is less-than and better suited to what we do after class. But, if my own story about my Ph.D. work is true, those emotional responses to learning can deter future growth. Even writing this chapter has been difficult; I worry if it will be good enough. I wonder if it will be dismissed as "that feminist stuff."

I leave you with these final questions. First, how can we debunk the myth that reason and intellect are at the heart of education? What other binaries limit transformative teaching and learning? And, perhaps most important, how does my own emotional self affect, prohibit, nurture, and/or transform my educational self?

LAURA BOLF-BELIVEAU

Laura Bolf-Beliveau, Ph.D., is a professor of English at the University of Central Oklahoma where she regularly teaches classes in secondary methods, young adult literature, multicultural women's writing, and first year composition. She is a former high school teacher with over 15 years of experience in urban, rural, and suburban districts. In addition to publications in the areas of social justice, identity, and feminism, Bolf-Beliveau has given numerous national presentations about young adult literature, media integration, and argumentative writing. She was a team leader and writer of Oklahoma's ELA standards. Additionally, she has worked on numerous Oklahoma Regent's grants (as co-PI and facilitator). In addition to winning the Neely Excellence in Teaching Award in 2017, she has been awarded College of Liberal Arts Outstanding Teaching Award, Vanderford Teaching Award, Herbert S. Dordick Award for Outstanding Mentorship, and the College of Education and Professional Studies Collaborative Teamwork Award.

COLLECTIVE WISDOM

The neuroscience of education tells us that the brain that does the work does the learning, speaking colloquially of course. These bits of collected wisdom are from the stories where you will get the full sense of the transformations of the authors. If, however, you are rushing or seeking a reminder of those stories, then these brief comments will benefit you. Consider these as points for reflection, as it is in the reflective moments that transformation and learning occur. Perhaps Dr. Neely would suggest that we open our minds and think.

- **Insights from the Foreword:**

  1. Extremely important to me were gentle inputs from my mentors: my father, mother, grocery store owner, clarinet teacher and other select teachers. My father only had a high school diploma. However, each night he would study by himself; I watched.

  2. Soon, fear of failure begins to obstruct learning. Failure is a big important part of learning and freedom. It is important to be given the opportunity and to take the right to fail.

  3. Encouragement and guidance can only be heard and understood when it is personal. It is helpful at times to set up a manageable project so that success is likely. Nothing is more stimulating and encouraging than success. We learn things two ways—intellectually and emotionally. Intellectual learning is rapid but tends to be external. Emotional learning takes

longer, is personal, and can be refined.

- **Insights from the Introduction:**

    4. Gritch refers to speech acts that include complaints, excuses, griping, blaming, and whining; a no-gritch mentality is a sign of resilience and steadfast persistence in learning.[1]

- **Insights from Chapter 1:**

    5. Learn from the guides along the way, because I firmly believe that we can learn from anyone. It may be that after observing others, we choose to learn from them but select another path to our personal success.

    6. Through service learning and field experiences, students share that many beliefs that they held about diverse populations are simply not true and they start to question themselves, modifying their personal philosophy to be more open.

- **Insights from Chapter 2:**

    7. During my educational career of over 30 years, I have adopted a three-part, student-centered, transformative learning strategy, which is deeply rooted in Chinese culture— a part of my ethnic heritage—and in the teaching philosophies of Confucius.

    8. I often design and assign projects to students requiring experiments or simulations to acquire knowledge, either independently or with teamwork. I believe that this hands-on experience gives my students a competitive edge in their future professional careers and graduate education.

- **Insights from Chapter 3:**

    9. Give yourself permission to engage constantly in imperfect trials; risk the perfect outcome to gain new learning experiences.

    10. For all learners and, in particular, for learners with salient African American or female identities, my presence as a fellow learner, researcher, professor, and dean matters. This is

especially true if I remain a learner who is willing to share challenges experienced while finding her own movement.

- **Insights from Chapter 4:**

  11. Inside/Outside Learning and Teaching can predispose one to diversity and tolerant thinking when confronted by radically different learning environments.

  12. Being a faculty member in the classroom posed different positions. I was leader and authority in the class organization. While I treasured my status, I never flouted nor violated; I had learned productive interactions from cherished professors who formed my understanding of the teaching and learning enterprise as a faculty member.

- **Insights from Chapter 5:**

  13. These experiences, among people from different locales, have taught me a central lesson about learning, which is that it often requires a different framework of mind to begin the learning process, one that is freer of preconceptions. The idea of examining one's own assumptions is a key part of this lesson.

  14. ...he responded by noting that he had "a comfort with uncertainty."...This idea is, in my opinion, the essence of learning: to distinguish the process of discovery from extant (and assumed) knowledge.[5] This requires crossing a cognitive bridge from a process of just gathering together existing knowledge to one that generates new knowledge.

- **Insights from Chapter 6:**

  15. The time studying with her was one of the most transformational experiences in my life. I learned that each person has a choice on which attitude and road to take, no matter how brutally fate may intervene.

  16. "Failures" under these conditions are, in reality, experiences towards personal and professional growth. The expectation that learning is supposed to be "easy" bears a multitude of frustrating experiences.

- ## Insights from Chapter 7:

  17. Each year the students in your freshman classroom are generally around 18-years old and you are $(n + 1)$ years old, where n is the age you were when you first started teaching. The cultural and societal connections between you and the students in your classroom become more of a generation gap each year. Every year you adjust.

  18. How else to best help students on their journey? I have come to understand that teaching students *how to learn* is the most important thing I can teach them.

- ## Insights from Chapter 8:

  19. In my second year of college, my English got better and I set my goal to learn and succeed no matter what the obstacles were, and most importantly, I learned how to manage my time.

  20. In order to conquer our biases, both implicit and explicit, we have to first become aware of them and then actively work to dismantle them by communication and interaction with each other.

- ## Insights from Chapter 9:

  21. Students must be aware of the processes and the reasons for various procedures used in the classroom, as well as, outside assignments that may require interpretation, research, analysis and integration.

  22. Not only is it important to offer a transformational approach to study and learning in the classroom, but it is equally important to be involved with the students to help aid in their success.

- ## Insights from Chapter 10:

  23. *There is no substitute for good people believing in you.* All the technology and computer programs in the world pale in comparison to what happens between people when such an interchange occurs. And more, in my opinion, technology can

significantly get in the way: it can minimize the human-to-human factor that I believe is necessary for most transformative experiences.

24. Transformative learning (is there any other kind?) involves a change in thinking, feeling, and behaving that is maintained long enough to replace an old way of being with a new one. It is not a superficial experience but one that strikes deep into the person's perceptual system and stimulates alteration and difference. It is the difference that actually makes a difference that is observable.

- ## Insights from Chapter 11:

25. The bubble is the world of opportunity where you are shielded in a sense from the outside world. In this bubble, it's ok if everyone is unique and doesn't do or think the same. This is what enriches our experiences and what we thrive upon to make it interesting and to challenge us. In the academia bubble, we encourage and strive for diversity rather than hiding from it.

26. Watching them grow from freshman to graduates is inspiring. As I see students maturing, mentoring other students, taking leadership roles, and becoming successful practitioners—this is a sign of success for me. I have done my job when I see even a glimmer of that love of life-long learning I hold so significant.

- ## Insights from Chapter 12:

27. The process of being transformed by my experiences are important for me to share with students about how important the family is to each member and society as a whole.

28. I know a student's environment affects their ability and willingness to learn, so I try to provide a "user friendly" environment where all students are challenged in a supportive atmosphere and they want to learn. Human dignity and diversity must be respected in everything we teach and model.

- **Insights from Chapter 13:**

  29. In the teaching of writing, too, sometimes I think that my primary goal is to get students to write sentences that they didn't know they would write—to surprise themselves.

  30. This model of creative group interaction is part of what I'm trying to do in the classroom, especially when I'm trying to figure out which questions will provoke students into good discussion. Once I've gotten a student or two to respond, then I can take their responses and run with them, spinning off new questions or maybe even an impromptu activity that has used the ideas they have come up with in that class discussion.

- **Insights from Chapter 14:**

  31. I understand from my own experiences the importance of health and wellness to the learning process and the importance of *social support* to a basic sense of health and wellness.

  32. We all can remain aware that students are learning in the midst of a *life*—a life that can detract from the basic sense of health and wellness that is needed for learning to take place. We can recognize that in critical moments of the learning journey, an amount of social support in one form or another can make the difference between students' success and failure.

- **Insights from Chapter 15:**

  33. I had assumed that science was a body of knowledge, but somewhere I had completely missed that science is *also* a process humans use to make sense of the world around them. It is a process in which people seek out explanations for questions; the seeking is just as much the science (or more so) as the knowing.

  34. However, what if we changed our mindset as teachers to embrace not telling students answers? What if we searched

for "Aha!" moments that lead to realized ignorance in our students? Not that we are purposely trying to make our students feel inferior, but what if we spent our own preparation time working on the questions of our own discipline that would cause students to rethink what they know?

- **Insights from Chapter 16:**

35. Questions posed by Dr. Bain caused me to think deeply and reflect about why and how topics are covered in the classroom. Often this reflection led me to make changes, not necessarily in the material covered, but how it was presented. I have come to understand different students may learn in different ways and often there are several ways that are effective when it comes to how people learn.

36. Now I often stop during the presentation to ask questions that lead to the students using what they know to discover the answers for themselves. This subtle, but important shift, engages the students and allows them to think more deeply about the subject, so they learn from that experience.

- **Insights from Chapter 17:**

37. I now use such storytelling techniques in my own classes because of him. I was transformed by this technique of critical creativity. To this day, I require in almost all my classes that my students be creative as they rewrite, revise, and rethink the art of narratives.

38. I have become the teachers I have learned from by mirroring their lessons and by sharing their pedagogical creativity with my students. Therefore, death dies as life is reborn while experiencing a shared dream luminating each other.

- **Insights from Chapter 18:**

39. I realized that the secret ("aha!" moment) was to reach Maslow's higher/hierarchical order of intrinsic motivation. That is, to achieve our potential, reach self-actualization, and experience fulfillment.

40. Learning in the 21ˢᵗ century is no longer limited to just a physical classroom in a brick-and-mortar university. Today's digital learners, who live and learn in an immersive environment, prefer learning to occur in a virtual space or outside the classroom. Likewise, non-traditional students with full-time jobs also prefer learning and just-in-time skill acquisition without time and location constraints.

- **Insights from Chapter 19:**

41. No longer silenced and cast out, but not yet fully integrated into an institutional culture that we both claim and question, LGBTQ+ faculty members have the opportunity—and, I believe, the obligation—to cultivate an uncomfortable but fruitful middle ground, planting and nurturing the seeds of the world we seek to create for ourselves and for our students.

42. Acknowledging and discussing our different, but otherwise unacknowledged, subject positions are essential first steps in building the bridges that will carry us beyond familiar and often stereotyped modes of thinking and reveal new ways of understanding ourselves and our world.

- **Insights from Chapter 20:**

43. I gathered from interviews and observations of faculty that some of the success of the program was due to team research and collaborations over international conferences. Professors in Poland have heavy teaching and research loads. The sense of unity in the department was strong, something I was pleased to observe. I did not observe factions, bullying or any such behaviors, but rather a strong network of scholars working together.

44. Investigating the culture you are going to live in is of the utmost importance, including basic pronunciation of names and greetings. Studying the geo-politics of the region will be most helpful for understanding the culture in which you are going to live.

- **Insights from Chapter 21:**

45. I am convinced that students learn best when they seek answers to questions they pose themselves, and the best questions are those for which no one yet knows the answer. The best measure of success in my classroom is when students ask me questions I can't answer, and in fact, sometimes no one has yet answered.

46. I have a passion for helping students notice the world around them, and I tirelessly work to increase their powers of observation. Although many students are "visual" learners, most students come into plant biology classes unaware that they are suffering from "plant blindness." They do not have well-developed powers of observation.

- **Insights from Chapter 22:**

47. If we only do what we have seen others do, we will never do things in new ways, or improve upon how things are done. It is important to add our personal insights to how we do things. I have found that a little bit of reflection can help me understand what skills and talents I have and how I can apply them to new situations.

48. I have been working in universities for over twenty years, but I still have more to learn. This inquisitive dissatisfaction drives me to seek opportunities to better understand higher education and student learning. It has broadened my reading beyond the chemical literature, and it has pushed me to interact with more people from across my institution and beyond.

- **Insights from Chapter 23:**

49. So, emotions are vital to transformative learning. They need a place to go—this third space. Once there, all classroom participants must be reflexive—cognizant of their own beliefs while open to discovery of others.

50. Previously in this chapter, I stated that emotions are always present in teaching and learning. What we **do** with them affects our educational transformation. "Do" is the important word in this claim: for transformative teaching and learning to take place, participants must do—must engage, debate, listen, speak, think, etc. Active engagement within a third space can produce effects that move classrooms from passive to active.

REFERENCES

Introduction

[1]Sims, J., Cunliff, E., Sims, A., & Robertson, K. (2018). *Probing leadership from racio-ethnic perspectives in higher education: An emergent model of accelerating leader identity.* In Jean Lau Chin, Joseph E. Trimble, and Joseph E. Garcia (Eds.), Global and culturally diverse leaders and leadership: New dimensions and challenges for business, education, and society (pp. 183-209). Bingley, UK: Emerald.

Chapter 3: Jeanetta D. Sims

[1]Sims, J. D. (2011). A muted voice on holy ground: Reflections on the dialectics experienced as an African American female professor in a Christian university. In M. N. Niles and N. S. Gordon (Eds)., *Still searching for our mothers' gardens: Experiences of new, tenure-track women of color at 'majority' institutions (pp. 21–40).* Lanham, MD: University Press of America; and Sims, J. D. *(in press).* No gentlemen's agreement here: Higher education reflections on being womanist and the dialectics present in an African American Woman's Administrative Journey. In J. Cubbage (Ed.), *Developing women leaders in the academy through enhanced communication strategies.* Lanham, MD: Lexington Books.

[2]Sims, J. D. (2014, April). Center for Excellence in Transformative Teaching & Learning TeTalk: *Collaborative teaching.* Retrieved from https://www.youtube.com/watch?v=RHqGis7M_Gc&feature=youtu.be; and Sims, J. D., Neese, A., & Glidden, T. (2016). Collaborative teaching through co-creation in marketing education: A customer-centric approach to transformative learning. *Marketing Management Association Fall Conference Proceedings,* 46–47.

[3]Sims, J., Shuff, J., Neese, S., Lai, H.-L., Lim, O. F., & Neese, A. (2016). Diverse student scholars: How a faculty member's undergraduate research program can advance workforce diversity learning. In C. L. Scott and J. D. Sims (Eds.), *Expanding workforce diversity programs, curriculum, and degrees in higher education* (pp. 62–73). Hershey, PA: IGI Global; and Sims, J. D., Doré, A., Vo, M., Lai, H-L., & Lim, O. F. (2018). Diverse Student Scholars: A five-

faceted model of student transformation from embedded research mentorship in marketing courses. *Scholarship and Practice of Undergraduate Research, 2*(1), 33–42.

Chapter 5: John F. Barthell

[1]Bacon, F. (1994). *Novum organum.* (Translated by P. Urbach and J. Gibson.) Chicago and LaSalle, IL: Open Court.

[2]Fleck, L. (1979). *Genesis and development of a scientific fact.* (Translated by F. Bradley and T. J. Trenn.). Chicago, IL: The University of Chicago Press.

[3]Kuh, G. D. (2008). *High-impact educational practices: What they are, who has access to them, and why they matter.* Washington, DC: Association of American Colleges and Universities.

[4]Medawar, P. B. (1979). *Advice to a young scientist.* New York, NY: Basic Books.

[5]Wenner, A. M. (1989). Concept-centered versus organism-centered biology. *Integrative and Comparative Biology*, 29, 1177–1197.

[6]Karukstis, K. K., & Elgren, T. E. (Eds). (2007). Developing and sustaining a research-supportive curriculum: A compendium of successful practices. Washington, DC: The Council on Undergraduate Research.

[7]Barthell, J., Cunliff, E., Gage, K., Radke, W., & Steele, C. (2010). Transformative learning: Collaborating to enhance student learning. *Proceedings from the 115th Annual Meeting of NCA/The Higher Learning Commission*, 26:56–60.

[8]Gentile, J., Brenner, K., & Stephens, A. (Eds). (2017). *Undergraduate Research Experiences for STEM Students: Successes, Challenges, and Opportunities.* National Academies Press, Washington, DC.

[9]Barthell, J., Pope, M., King, J., Verschelden, C., Hughes, C., & Wilson, G. (2014). Using a transformative learning transcript to assess high-impact practices. *Proceedings from the 119th Annual Meeting of NCA/The Higher Learning Commission.* 30:58–63.

[10]Springer, M. S., Barthell, J. F., Simmons, C. K., Jackson-Hardwick, D., & Wilson, G. M. (2018). Broadening campus participation in undergraduate research through the office of high-impact practices. *Scholarship and Practice of Undergraduate Research*, 1, 69–75.

Chapter 13: Matthew Hollrah

[1]Freire, P. (2005). *Pedagogy of the oppressed*. (30th Anniversary Ed.). New York, NY: Continuum.

Chapter 14: Christy Vincent

[1]Silverman, D. C., Underhile, R., & Keeling, R. (2008). Student health reconsidered: A radical proposal for thinking differently about health-related programs and services for students. *Student Health Spectrum*, 4–11.

[2]House, J. S. (1981). *Work stress and social support*. Reading, MA: Addison-Wesley.

[3]House, J. S. (1981). *Work stress and social support*. Reading, MA: Addison-Wesley; and House, J. S., & Kahn, R. L. (1985). Measures and concepts of social support. In S. Cohen & S. L. Syme (Eds.), *Social support and health (pp. 83-108)*. Orlando: Academic Press.

[4]Cohen, S., Underwood, L. G., & Gottlieb, B. H. (2000). *Social support measurement and intervention: A guide for health and social scientists*. Oxford University Press.

[5]Silverman, D. C., Underhile, R., & Keeling, R. (2008). Student health reconsidered: A radical proposal for thinking differently about health-related programs and services for students. *Student Health Spectrum*, 4–11.

[6]Chao, R. C. L. (2012). Managing perceived stress among college students: The roles of social support and dysfunctional coping. *Journal of College Counseling*, 15, 5–21; and Henninger IV, W. R., Eshbaugh, El M., Osbeck, A., & Madigan, C. (2016). Perceived social support and roommate status and predictors of college student loneliness. *Journal of College and University Student Housing*, 42, 46–59; and Mattanah, J. F., Brooks, L. J., Brand, B. L.,

Quimby, J. L., & Ayers, J. F. (2012). A social support intervention and academic achievement in college: Does perceived loneliness mediate the relationship? *Journal of College Counseling*, 15, 22–36; and Zavatkay, D. (2015). Social support and community college student academic persistence. *Proceedings from the NERA Conference 2015*. Paper 3 http://digitalcommons.uconn.edu/nera-2015/3

[7]*Learning Reconsidered: A campus-wide focus on the student experience*. NASPA and the American College Personnel Association (ACPA), 2004.

[8]Zavatkay, D. (2015). Social support and community college student academic persistence. *Proceedings from the NERA Conference 2015*. Paper 3 http://digitalcommons.uconn.edu/nera-2015/3

Chapter 15: Daniel Vincent

[1]Bennett, T. (2013). *Teacher proof: Why research in education doesn't always mean what it claims, and what you can do about it*. Routledge, NY.

[2]Brown, P., Roediger III, H., & McDaniel, M. (2014). *Make it stick: the science of successful learning*. Cambridge, MA: The Belknap Press of Harvard University Press.

[3]Brookfield, S., & Preskill, S. (2005). *Discussion as a way of teaching: Tools and techniques for democratic classrooms, 2nd ed*. San Francisco, CA: Josey-Bass.

[4]Rothstein, D., & Santana, L. (2015). *Make just one change: Teach students to ask their own questions*. Cambridge, MA: Harvard Education Press.

Chapter 16: David Bass

[1]Bain, K. (2004). *What the best college teachers do*. Cambridge, MA: Harvard University Press.

Chapter 17: Wayne Stein

[1]The metaphor of dreaming within this narrative comes from: Dalai Lama. "8 Stages of Dissolutions." From the *Third Art of Dying Conference*, March 2000. https://sites.google.com/site/capucinehenrydalailama/8-stages-of-dissolution.

Chapter 18: Joselina Cheng
[1]Collins, J. (2001). *Good to great*. New York, NY: HarperCollins Publishers.

Chapter 19: J. David Macey
[1]Norton, R. (1974). The homosexual literary tradition: Course outline and objectives. *College English*, *35*(6), 674–678, 687–692.

[2]Turner, V. (1969). *The ritual process: Structure and anti-structure*. Chicago, IL: Aldine Publishing Co.

[3]Mezirow, J. (1996). Contemporary paradigms of learning. *Adult education quarterly*, *46*(3), 158–173.

[4]Anzaldúa, G. (2012). *Borderlands/la frontera: The new mestiza* (4th ed.). San Francisco, CA: Aunt Lute Books.

[5]Anzaldúa, G. (2002). (Un)natural bridges, (un)safe spaces. In G. Anzaldúa & A. Keating, Eds., *This bridge we call home: Radical visions for transformation* (pp. 1–5). New York, NY: Routledge.

[6]Anzaldúa, G. (1983). Foreword to the second edition. In C. Moraga & G. Anzaldúa, Eds., *This bridge called my back: Writings by radical women of color* (2nd ed., pp. iv-v). New York, NY: Kitchen Table–Women of Color Press.

[7]Blake, W. (1979). The marriage of heaven and hell. In M. L. Johnson & J. E. Grant, Eds., *Blake's poetry and designs* (pp. 84–102). New York, NY: W. W. Norton & Co.

Chapter 21: Gloria Caddell
[1]Wandersee, J. H., & Schussler, E. E. (1999). Preventing plant blindness. *The American Biology Teacher*, *61*(2), 82–86.

Chapter 23: Laura Bolf-Beliveau
[1]Boler, M. (1999). *Feeling power: Emotions and education*. New York: Routledge.

[2]Leavy, P., & Harris, A. (2019). *Contemporary feminist research from theory to practice*. New York, NY: The Guilford Press.

[3]Leavy, P., & Harris, A. (2019). *Contemporary feminist research from theory to practice*. New York, NY: The Guilford Press.

INDEX

ABOUT THE EDITORS

Jeanetta D. Sims, Ph.D., APR

Dr. Jeanetta D. Sims is an award-winning educator, researcher, and professor at the University of Central Oklahoma, where she teaches business communication and marketing communications courses and is accredited in public relations. Along with serving as dean of the Jackson College of Graduate Studies, she is a transformative learning scholar. Through her undergraduate research initiative, Diverse Student Scholars, she has made more than 80 research presentations and mentored more than 40 funded student grants involving university students. Sims' co-edited book publications include Mentoring Undergraduate Research and Developing Workforce Diversity Programs, Curriculum, and Degrees in Higher Education. She is a co-editor of the *Journal of Transformative Learning* and the *Transformative Learning Conference Proceedings*.

Ed Cunliff, Ph.D.

Dr. Ed Cunliff is an innovative and reflective educator who facilitates organizational and individual growth. He teaches courses in program evaluation and transformative learning as a professor of adult and higher education in the College of Education and Professional Studies at the University of Central Oklahoma. Cunliff is a co-editor of the *Journal of Transformative Learning* and the *Transformative Learning Conference Proceedings*.

Anna Doré

Anna Doré is a graduate student at the University of Central Oklahoma, where she is pursuing a master's degree in creative writing. Since 2018, she has served as an editorial research assistant for the *Journal of Transformative Learning* and the *Transformative Learning Conference Proceedings*.